Praise for

The Marshall Plan
for Novel Writing

"Like the Marshall Plan of 1948, this Marshall Plan offers hope! The manual is a simple and effective road map for all new and aspiring writers. Definitely user-friendly."

—Lori Copeland, best-selling author of *With This Ring* and *The Courtship of Cade Kolby*

"A clear and extremely readable guide to writing. While *The Marshall Plan* may not be able to guarantee a sale, it will certainly put a writer on the right track."

—Jennifer Sawyer Fisher, senior editor, Avon Books

"*The Marshall Plan for Novel Writing* is a master plan for aspiring novelists. Evan Marshall is brilliant."

—Bobbi Smith, best-selling author of *Outlaw's Lady*

"A comprehensive manual to writing a novel for all writers—from the beginner to the more advanced looking for polishing tips. Savvy and concise."

—Bill Contardi, literary agent, William Morris Agency

"*The Marshall Plan* is *the* bible for every aspiring novelist. More than an essential tool, Evan Marshall's definitive, step-by-step guide strips away the secrets of character, plot and content. In short, he gives you the recipes for writing a novel that'll sell. He'll have you cookin' in no time."
> —Judith Gould, New York Times best-selling author of *Sins*, *Second Love* and *Till the End of Time*

"Finally, a practical how-to manual for all aspiring authors, written with wit and wisdom. A delightful read!"
> —Maureen Walters, vice president, Curtis Brown, Ltd.

"Brilliant. *The Marshall Plan for Novel Writing* presents a fail-safe approach to a first novel, providing the building blocks and the polishing tools an inexperienced writer needs to produce a salable manuscript."
> —Candace Robb, best-selling author of the *Owen Archer* mysteries

"An invaluable tool for the aspiring novelist. An upbeat, easy-to-follow guide that takes the mystery out of writing."
> —Alicia Condon, editorial director of Leisure Books/Love Spell

The Marshall Plan for
NOVEL WRITING

The Marshall Plan for

NOVEL WRITING

A 16-step program guaranteed to take you
from idea to completed manuscript.

Evan Marshall

WRITER'S DIGEST BOOKS
CINCINNATI, OHIO

Other fine Writer's Digest Books are available from your local bookstore or direct from the publisher.

Visit our Web site at www.writersdigest.com for information on more resources for writers.

To receive a free weekly E-mail newsletter delivering tips and updates about writing and about Writer's Digest products, send an E-mail with the message "Subscribe Newsletter" to newsletter-request@writersdigest.com, or register directly at our Web site at www.writersdigest.com.

06   05   04   7 6 5

Library of Congress has catalogued hardcover edition as follows:

Marshall, Evan.
   The Marshall plan for novel writing / Evan Marshall.—1st ed.
      p.   cm.
   Includes index.
   ISBN 0-89879-848-5 (hardcover)
   1. Fiction—Authorship. I. Title.
PN3365.M28   1998
808.3—dc21   98-35710
ISBN 1-58297-062-9 (pbk.: alk. paper)   CIP

Edited by Jack Heffron
Production Edited by Michelle Kramer
Cover Designed by David Mill of Design Mill

About the Author

Evan Marshall is the president of The Evan Marshall Agency, a leading literary agency that specializes in representing fiction writers. A former book editor and packager, he has contributed articles on writing and publishing to *Writer's Digest* and other magazines. He is the author of *Eye Language* and a forthcoming series of mystery novels. He lives in Pine Brook, New Jersey.

Acknowledgments

Special thanks

At Writer's Digest Books: to my editor, Jack Heffron, for his insight and intelligence; and to Bill Brohaugh for his longtime commitment to this project. I am also grateful to the following people for their invaluable contributions: Stacie Berger, Christine Carli, Julia Groh, Richard Hunt, Michelle Kramer, David Mill of Design Mill, Angie Philpott, Ruth Preston, Mert Ransdell, Brian Roeth, Budge Wallis and Joanne Widmer.

At The Evan Marshall Agency: to Nancy Bandel for her loyal support, and to my clients for all they have taught me.

At home: to my wife, Martha Jewett, and our sons, Justin Marshall and Warren Marshall, for their love and understanding.

Genius only means an infinite capacity for taking pains.

JANE ELLICE HOPKINS,
WORK AMONGST WORKING MEN

Table of Contents

Introduction 1

How the Plan Works 3

Part 1   **PLANNING FOR SUCCESS**

STEP 1   Finding the Perfect Novel for You 6

STEP 2   Shaping Your Story Idea 15

STEP 3   Creating Your Lead 28

STEP 4   Defining Your Other Characters 40

Part 2   **YOUR COMPLETE GUIDE TO PLOTTING**

STEP 5   Getting Off to the Right Start 55

STEP 6   Interweaving Story Lines 83

STEP 7   Surprising the Reader 105

STEP 8   Ending on All the Right Notes 112

Part 3   **HOW TO WRITE FICTION LIKE A PRO**

STEP 9   Putting It All Together 128

STEP 10   Mastering the Modes I:
          Action, Summary, Dialogue 142

STEP 11   Mastering the Modes II: Feelings/
          Thoughts and Background 157

STEP 12   Completing a Draft 166

Part 4   **POLISHING YOUR MANUSCRIPT**

STEP 13   How to Be Your Own Editor 178

STEP 14   Applying the Finishing Touches 189

Part 5   **MARKETING YOUR NOVEL**

STEP 15   Producing a Knockout Proposal 194

STEP 16   Approaching Agents and Editors 201

Glossary 219

Appendix: A Sample Synopsis 223

Index 235

Introduction

As I look back on years of participating in writers' conferences around the country, one in particular stands out. It was an important event, sponsored by a national writers' organization, and a number of heavy hitters—writers, agents and editors—were scheduled to speak.

I had some free time before my workshop, so I sat in on a talk by a New York editor with whom I had done considerable business. Her workshop topic, as listed in the conference brochure, was "Novel Writing 101: A Hands-On Approach."

Her presentation was certainly thorough. She covered such topics as dialogue, viewpoint and characterization in admirable detail. But when she was finished speaking and opened the floor for questions, everyone in the audience just sat there looking confused.

Finally a man raised his hand. "That's all well and good," he said, "but how do you know when to do each of those things?"

The editor paused, clearly struggling for an answer. At last she replied, "Well, you do them all at the same time."

A woman near me threw down her notebook in exasperation. I couldn't blame her. The editor's answer hadn't been helpful at all. If you ask me, her approach wasn't hands-on, it was hands-off!

Later, taking a break in my hotel room, I wondered how I would have answered that man's question. I *could* have answered it, but it would have been a long answer!

It then occurred to me that he wouldn't have asked the question in the first place if the editor had presented her material differently, if she had put the process of creating a novel into linear, step-by-step form—told what to do when—instead of suggesting a literary juggling act.

If you ask a painter how she creates a landscape, her reply would resemble the editor's: She does everything at the same time. She blocks in the sky, roughs in the foreground, works on the middle distance, adds detail to the foreground, refines the sky and so on. She *is* doing everything at the same time—in a manner of speaking. But it's physically impossible for her brush to be in two places at once.

And so it is with a novel. It's physically impossible to work on dialogue, viewpoint, characterization and all the other aspects of writing a novel at the same time. When the process is broken down into its steps, it's clear that creating a novel is, in fact, a linear process.

It's this process I have presented in my seminars and workshops since that day in my hotel room when I realized that it's what beginning novelists really need. And it's this process I will share with you.

This book is different from other guides because of its step-by-step format. It also addresses novel writing in a new way. You'll find terminology and definitions here that you've never seen before.

Perhaps because I'm an agent and make my living solely by selling books (most of them novels), my method takes a highly practical approach. You'll target a genre for your novel, then develop your story idea and characters with this genre's requirements firmly in mind. The hardest part of writing a novel is finishing it, and to make sure you do, you'll use a special template to plan your entire story—subplots and all—before you even start writing. You'll translate your completed templates into professional-quality text. Finally, you'll create a dynamic selling proposal for your novel and approach agents and editors with maximum effectiveness.

As a literary agent, I have helped dozens and dozens of writers achieve success with this method. Beginning writers bursting with ideas but unsure how to turn them into novels have found guidance in this methodical, "left-brain" process. Published writers who always wrote "instinctively," discovering their novels as they went along, have used this method to diagnose and repair ailing manuscripts. In all cases, these writers have been rewarded with compliments from editors on the writers' mastery of their craft—and with publication.

I hope *The Marshall Plan for Novel Writing* does that for you.

How the Plan Works

Because each step in my system builds on what you have already accomplished, it's important to follow the steps in order. The following sections give an overview of the parts that make up the plan.

PART 1: PLANNING FOR SUCCESS

Part I shows you how to lay the groundwork for a solid novel. You discover the kind of novel that's perfect for *you* to write, then develop a story idea that's original, powerful and suitable for the type of book you're writing. Part I then shows you how to use your story idea to create your novel's characters.

PART 2: YOUR COMPLETE GUIDE TO PLOTTING

This part takes you through the planning of your story. You begin by ascertaining the ideal length for your novel. You learn about sections, the units of action and reaction that constitute your story, and about section sheets, on which you'll plan your sections. Part II then takes you through the plotting of your novel's sections. You devise subordinate story lines and interweave them with your main story line, plant three vital story twists, and plot your novel's last sections for maximum impact.

PART 3: HOW TO WRITE FICTION LIKE A PRO

This part shows you how to write the story you've plotted. You discover the secrets of viewpoint writing, then learn how to write action sections and reaction sections and create connectors—devices for linking sections. You conquer the five fiction modes: action, summary, dialogue, thoughts/feelings and background. Finally, part III addresses the act of writing, from setting up your work space to setting goals to setting up your manuscript.

PART 4: POLISHING YOUR MANUSCRIPT

This part guides you in revising and editing your completed manuscript. You use the Novelist's Manual for Self-Editing to bulletproof your story and perfect your language. Then you divide your novel into chapters; adjust your manuscript's length, if necessary; and give your book an intriguing title.

PART 5: MARKETING YOUR NOVEL

Often the first stage in submitting your novel to agents and editors is submitting a proposal for your novel. This part shows you how to create the most important element of the proposal: the synopsis, a powerful marketing tool. Then you begin the process of targeting agents and editors. Part V shows you how to attract these professionals' attention and get your novel in front of them for serious consideration.

APPENDIX: A SAMPLE SYNOPSIS

There's nothing like the real thing, and in the appendix you'll find an example of a strong synopsis for a novel that was ultimately sold and published.

Part 1

PLANNING FOR SUCCESS

In This Part . . .

This part helps you find your fiction niche, develop your story idea and create your characters.

Finding the Perfect Novel for You

In This Step
- Deciding what to write
- Targeting a genre

The writer—let's call her Anne—hurried through the restaurant to my table. "Thank you so much for seeing me," she said, shaking my hand and taking her seat.

"Barbara's right," I said, referring to my client who had referred Anne to me. "You're quite talented. But I have to be honest. I don't think I can sell your manuscript."

There was devastation in her eyes.

"Do you read a lot of literary novels?" I asked gently.

She looked down at the table. "No."

"Then why did you want to write one?"

She shrugged. "They're so popular now. I thought it was what editors were looking for."

"Barbara said you love romances."

She blushed as red as the tablecloth. "Well, yes—to *read*."

I smiled. "Wasn't it the beginning of a romance you gave Barbara to read?"

"Oh, that. I was just fooling around."

"Why fool around? If you love romances, write one."

She stared at me, enlightenment dawning. "You know," she said, her eyes aglow, "that *was* the most wonderful idea for a love story. . . ."

"Tell me about it," I said.

One year later, I met Anne for lunch again. She wanted to meet at the same restaurant.

"Thank you," she said, handing me a manila envelope. In it was a contract I had sent her to sign, a contract for a romance—the one she'd told me about—to be published by a leading New York publisher.

She raised her glass to mine. "To your invaluable advice."

"To your success," I said.

A COMMON MISTAKE

Anne is not unusual. Many people, when they decide to write a novel, have no idea what to write. They just want to get published, so they choose what looks easiest or is currently hot.

Some decide on young-adult novels. After all, they reason, these stories are shorter and simpler than adult novels, so they must be easier to write, right? Wrong. If anything, they're harder because they telescope plot and emotion onto a smaller canvas.

Others choose romances. Why? They follow a formula; anyone can churn out one of those, right? Wrong. Romance is impossible to fake. Editors and readers can spot an insincere effort a mile away.

Other would-be novelists have their own ideas of what looks easy; they turn out books they shouldn't be writing because they are not familiar enough with the genre and have no passion for it. These insincere efforts are inevitably inferior and therefore don't sell. At this point, these people turn in frustration to some other kind of book that looks easy, hoping *it* will open the door to publication. And on it goes.

In good writing, nothing's easy. That's the first truth you have to accept. Once you do, you're ready to make an informed, intelligent decision about the kind of book you should write. You should hone your craft on this kind of book instead of splashing about directionless in a sea of genres. It's this kind of book you'll have the best chance of selling.

THE RIGHT CHOICE

So what should you write? It's been right in front of you all the time: what you love to read.

Why should you write what you love to read? First, because you've read books in a specific genre for so long, you're aware of the kinds of stories that have been written in it. You also have a good idea of what works and what doesn't. Second, your passion as a reader will translate into passion as a writer.

So what do you love to read? What kinds of novels do you gravitate to in the bookstore or library? Who are your favorite authors? If, like many avid readers, you enjoy more than one genre, which is your favorite?

You may be unsure what genre your favorite books fall into. Maybe you choose more by author—you enjoy a writer's work and haven't given any thought to its genre. Nevertheless, as a novelist you must know exactly what genre or subgenre you're targeting. Years ago publishers maintained a "midlist" for novels that didn't quite fit genre criteria yet weren't "big" enough to be published at the top of the list. But in today's sophisticated market of superclassification, the midlist is gone, and every novel must fit into a niche.

Editors think in terms of genre when they acquire books, mostly from agents, who think the same way when they take on books from authors, who need to think this way too. Many writers resist categorizing their novels, insisting it will stifle their creativity. But a novel written without a genre in mind can be difficult if not impossible to sell. Challenge yourself to be creative within your genre's conventions.

To help you pinpoint your favorite genre, I've compiled the following list of fiction classifications and subclassifications, whether now or previously popular.

Action/Adventure

Mercenary	War
Survivalist	

Christian

Biblical	Mystery
Contemporary	Mystery/Romance
Frontier Romance	Romance
Historical	

Fantasy

Alternate History	Magic Realism
Contemporary	Medieval
Dark	Military
Epic	Modern
Gay	Science
High	Sociological
Humorous	Speculative Science Fiction/ Fantasy
Lesbian	Traditional
Light	Urban

Gay/Lesbian

Coming-of-Age	Romance
Erotica	Science Fiction
Mystery	Suspense
Relationship	

Historical

Biographical	Multicultural
Family Saga	Prehistoric
Frontier	Saga
General	Western
Generational Saga	

Horror

Contemporary	Occult
Crime	Paranormal
Dark	Psychological
Erotica	Technological
Humorous	Traditional
Light	Urban
Modern	

Mainstream

Biographical	New Age

Crime   Occult
Erotica   Paranormal
Feminist   Political
Glitz and Glamour   Sequel to Classic
Humor/Satire   Speculative
Literary   Sports
Magic Realism   Supernatural
Military/War   Women's

Mystery

Amateur Detective   Hard-Boiled Detective
Biographical Historical   Historical
Comic Caper   Humorous
Courtroom/Trial   Literary
Cozy   Malice Domestic
Crime   Police Procedural
Dark   Private Detective
Espionage   Puzzle
Fact-Based Contemporary   Surrealistic
Fact-Based Historical

Romance

Americana   Mature Contemporary
Angel   Multicultural Contemporary
Edwardian   Multicultural Historical
Fantasy   Nurse
Futuristic   Regency
Georgian   Reincarnation
Ghost   Romantic Suspense
Gothic   Short Humorous
                                            Contemporary
Historical Romance   Short Sensual Contemporary
Inspirational Contemporary   Short Sweet Contemporary
Inspirational Historical   Time Travel
Long Sensual   Vampire
   Contemporary

Magic   Victorian
Mainstream Contemporary

Science Fiction

Adventure	Humorous
Alternative	Military
Anthropological/Genetic	Mystery-Related
Apocalyptic	Offbeat
Avant-Pop	Postmodern
Cyberpunk	Psychological
Cybertek	Religious
Dark Fantasy	Sociological
Darkly Humorous	Space Opera
Erotica	Speculative
Experimental	Steampunk
Fantasy	Surreal/Mood
Feminist	Time Travel
Futuristic	Traditional
Hard	Urban Horror
Harsh Parody	Weird
Horrific	

Suspense

Crime	Political Thriller
Domestic	Psychological
Erotic Thriller	Psychosexual Thriller
Espionage	Serial-Killer Thriller
Legal Thriller	Techno-Thriller
Medical Thriller	Thriller
Paranormal Thriller	Woman-in-Jeopardy

Western

Adult	Military
Biographical	Traditional
Fact-Based	

Young Adult

Adventure	Humor
Biographical	Mystery
Coming-of-Age	Mystery Romance
Contemporary	Problem
Ethnic	Romance
Fantasy	Science Fiction
Historical	Suspense
Horror	Western

Incredible, isn't it? You most likely found your favorite genre in the list. Write it down. It's the genre in which you should be writing.

ADAPTING TO THE CURRENT MARKET

What if you read in a genre that is no longer being published because it has gone out of fashion? Two examples are the gothic and the family saga. Fans of "extinct" genres like these buy books that were first published years ago and are still in print, or they buy old used books, or they borrow old books from the library. If you're one of these people, you may be unsure whether your favorite genre is still being published. To find out, you'll need to do some research.

First, go to a large bookstore and check the shelves for *new* titles in this genre. Next, visit the library and scan the new-fiction section. Then check the general shelves.

If, at either the library or the bookstore, you find books in this genre that have been published within the past two years (check the copyright page), you're in good shape. This is the genre you should write in, because you love reading it and publishers are buying it.

If, on the other hand, you find nothing in your genre that's been published within the past two years, you have some adapting to do. There's no point in writing what you love to read if no one's publishing it anymore. In order to write—and sell—what you love to read, you must change what you love to read. You can do this in either of two ways:

1. Switch to the genre's currently popular form, if such exists.
2. Switch to a similar genre that is still being published.

Here's how it works. Let's say you love horror novels—the paperback-original, "category" kind, with covers featuring things like skulls and ferocious dolls. You buy these books used, and your research tells you this kind of horror isn't being published these days. What do you do?

Start with option #1. Visit a large bookstore and your library, looking for recently published horror. You discover that horror is still being published, but the novels are longer and more sophisticated. Read a few of these books. If they appeal to you, switch to this currently popular form of horror as your target genre.

If they don't appeal to you, try option #2. Now you're looking for a "live" genre you like as much as the one you've been reading. The genres likeliest to fit the bill are those that share characteristics with the genre you're switching from. So you ask yourself what you like most about the horror novels you've been reading. You decide it's that they're (1) gory and (2) scary.

So look for a live genre that is gory and scary. How about serial-killer thrillers? They're certainly gory and scary. Read a few. If you like them, read more, and if you still like them, make serial-killer thrillers your new target genre.

If serial-killer thrillers don't thrill you, repeat the process until you find a genre you like enough to switch to. If you do switch, *keep reading.* You're trying to bring yourself up to speed as quickly as possible, so you can't read too much.

STAYING ON TARGET

Write your target genre in capital letters on a piece of paper and post it where you can see it easily from where you write. As you create your novel, you may become discouraged and feel tempted to give in to an old urge and cast about for something new—something easier or currently hot. If this happens, look hard at that piece of paper, remember that you targeted this genre for a good reason and *resist that urge.*

Stick with your target genre. When people ask you what you write, say, "I write _____s." Period. You're no longer splashing about in the sea of genres. You're happily aboard ship and ready to set sail—or should I say "sale"?

To Recap
- Write what you love to read.
- Target a live genre.
- Keep reading in your target genre.
- Stay committed to your target genre.

STEP 2

Shaping Your Story Idea

In This Step
- Sources of inspiration
- How to shape a story idea

Next time you're in a group of people, try an experiment. First announce a piece of good news. You'll get a positive, maybe even an enthusiastic, reaction, a "Congratulations" or "That's great" or "Good for you."

Then tell the group about something terrible that happened to you. Watch gazes snap to you; listen for "Oh my goodness!" and "How awful!" and "What did you do?" That last question will be on everyone's mind: How did you deal with the disaster; what did you do to make things right again?

THE CRISIS

We all love bad news. We'll take it over good news any day—as long as it's about someone else! That's why we watch TV news, read the tabloids, go to the movies—and read novels. We want to know how someone, perhaps someone just like us, gets out of a bad situation.

If you think about it, an effective story begins with a person faced with a terrible problem—a *crisis*—that turns his world upside down and forces him to take immediate action to set things right. Here are examples of such crises from some popular novels.

Young Cathy Dollanganger is locked away with her brothers and sisters in their grandmother's attic by their selfish mother.

(*FLOWERS IN THE ATTIC*, BY V.C. ANDREWS)

Martin Brody, chief of police in the beach resort town of Amity, discovers that a great white shark is feeding on swimmers.

(*JAWS*, BY PETER BENCHLEY)

Chris MacNeil's daughter, Regan, is possessed by the devil.

(*THE EXORCIST*, BY WILLIAM PETER BLATTY)

Hercule Poirot is asked to solve the murder of Mr. Ratchett, a fellow passenger on the Orient Express.

(*MURDER ON THE ORIENT EXPRESS*, BY AGATHA CHRISTIE)

Philip Ashley's beloved cousin Ambrose dies under suspicious circumstances—poisoned, perhaps, by his beautiful wife Rachel, with whom Philip now finds himself falling in love.

(*MY COUSIN RACHEL*, BY DAPHNE DU MAURIER)

BEGINNING TO DEFINE YOUR LEAD

To begin developing your story idea, you need a crisis to present to your story's main character—your *lead*. But what constitutes a crisis depends on who it's happening to.

Who is your lead? You need a rudimentary idea at this early stage: For instance, is it a man or a woman? An adult, teen or preteen?

Some genres have a gender requirement for the lead. For example, the lead in most types of romances must be a woman. The lead in a traditional Western must be a man.

Think about your target genre. Does it have such a gender requirement for the lead? If your target genre has no gender requirement and you've observed no predominance of male or female leads, you have a choice. Your decision will come down to whether you feel more comfortable writing about a male or a female lead.

Give the gender decision some serious thought: You'll no doubt feel more comfortable "getting inside the skin" of one than of the other. Some writers feel more natural writing about a lead of their own gender. Other writers have no difficulty portraying the opposite sex and even prefer it. There's no correct answer; choose what feels right. But it's a decision you must make now, before you can continue shaping your story idea.

Now think about your lead's age. All you have to decide now is whether he or she is an adult, a teen or a preteen. It's an easy decision: If you're writing a novel for adults, your lead must be an adult. If you're writing a novel for teens or preteens, your lead must be the age of your oldest target reader.

You now know the gender and at least the approximate age of your lead. Write this description, for example, "man," "woman" or "twelve-year-old boy," on a piece of paper.

"SUPPOSES" AND WHERE TO FIND THEM

Now, what would constitute a crisis for your lead as you have defined him or her so far? Here's where you start brainstorming to come up with crisis ideas, or what I call "Supposes."

Where do you find Supposes? Where other writers find them: everywhere.

Your Life

Most novelists start with their own lives. Often they draw from their careers. Robin Cook drew on his experience as a surgeon to come up with his Suppose for *Coma* and a string of other medical thrillers. Scott Turow has mined his background as an attorney for the Supposes behind *Presumed Innocent* and his subsequent legal novels. P.D. James worked in the Police and Criminal Law Departments of England's Home Office before conceiving the Supposes of her mysteries featuring police detective Adam Dalgliesh. Does *your* work life suggest an interesting Suppose?

Everyday experiences can spark Supposes. Once while I was visiting a sick friend at a large New York City hospital, I got off the elevator, and the doors closed before I realized I was on the wrong floor. The floor was under construction, a desolate landscape of exposed wires and girders. I pressed the elevator button, waited what seemed an eternity, and decided to look for the stairs. I started down the corridor, which was so dark I couldn't see my hands before my face. Groping along, I felt a door and opened it. There, in dim light from a distant window, sat row upon row of oversize jars containing all manner of human parts.

> Suppose a visitor to a large hospital happened upon the lair of a twisted murderer working from inside the hospital itself.

I don't really believe that's what I wandered into, but I've taken what happened to me and given it a twist. This Suppose is appropriate for a medical thriller, a serial-killer thriller or a horror novel.

Your Family

Did your parents meet in an interesting way? Has one of your siblings had an adventure or a disturbing episode? What about your grandparents? Your aunts? Your uncles? Your cousins? Your spouse? Your children?

A friend told me about his cousin who bought a large cactus from a home furnishings store and placed the plant in a corner of his living room. A few hours later the plant appeared to wiggle. Dismissing this as the product of overactive imaginations, the man and his wife went to bed—and woke to find their house crawling with tarantulas.

Your Friends

Have any of your friends had experiences that would make for interesting Supposes? Think about gossip you've heard. People from your neighborhood, your church or synagogue, your gym or health club, or organizations you belong to can be rich with Suppose material.

One of my relatives had a friend, a woman who worked in law enforcement in the South, who heard a rumor that her husband, a politician, was a member of the Ku Klux Klan.

Suppose a Southern police chief heard a rumor that her senator husband was a member of the Ku Klux Klan.

Your Co-Workers

Listen for intriguing stories at work. Clients, customers and associates are all potential sources. One of my business acquaintances had the misfortune to be sitting in a train where a man went on a shooting rampage, killing a passenger sitting directly in front of my acquaintance.

Suppose a man were shot by a mad gunman on a train.

The Media

Be on the lookout for true incidents with Suppose potential in newspapers and magazines, on TV and radio. National Public Radio once aired a story about two fishermen who found a dead hippopotamus in a creek in the Midwest.

Suppose the director of a wild-animal park arrived at work to discover that one of his prize animals had escaped.

Places You've Been

Fascinating stories abound at vacation spots, where people often emerge from their shells. Listen for ideas in airports, on planes and in hotels, restaurants, bars and museums. At a hotel in New York City, I heard about a couple who had stayed there a month before. They had dinner in the dining room, then the woman went upstairs to freshen her makeup. In her room a man waited in the darkness and strangled her.

Suppose a woman found a killer waiting for her in her hotel room, struggled with him and barely escaped alive.

Your Dreams

Keep pen and paper at your bedside for writing down dreams while they're fresh. Don't wait till morning, when they flee at first light.

Eavesdropping

We overhear the most amazing things. Not long ago on a bus I heard two female college students discussing a third young woman from their dorm who someone was "pranking." Each morning when the young woman left for class she left her radio on to discourage intruders. Each night when she returned to her room, she found her radio and lamp unplugged. Yet, to her knowledge, no one else had a key to her room.

> Suppose a young woman "pranked" herself to get attention, was found out, and then when someone started pranking her for real, no one believed her.

THE THREE CRISIS CRITERIA

Once you have a Suppose that intrigues you, you must test it against three criteria to see if it will work as the crisis for your lead.

1. The Crisis Must Be Genre Appropriate

In my agency we often receive novels whose crises are patently unsuited to the books' intended genres. For example, a novel intended for preteens began with the lead, a twelve-year-old boy, witnessing the brutal murder of his father, a CIA agent, by international terrorists. Another novel, intended as a legal thriller, began with the lead's wife leaving him—and that was the extent of the crisis. If these writers had read extensively in their genres and considered their Supposes in relation to what they'd read, they would have realized there was no way to make their Supposes work.

From your extensive reading, you should have a good idea of the kinds of Supposes that work in your target genre. Can you imagine reading a book in your target genre that incorporates your Suppose?

Often it's easier to ask, "Is my Suppose patently wrong for my target genre?" We have little trouble recognizing what *won't* work. For example, let's say your target genre is short sweet contemporary romance, your lead is a woman and you've come up with this Suppose:

Suppose a woman, while having the foundation dug for a new house, released the vengeful spirit of a man who was buried alive.

This Suppose is unquestionably wrong for a short sweet contemporary romance, and you'd know this from your reading. But perhaps you could work with this Suppose, shaping it so that it would work.

Start by identifying exactly what aspect or aspects of the Suppose make it inappropriate. In this case it's the vengeful spirit; its malevolence suggests a horror novel.

But you like the spirit part. Is there any way to make it work? Think about the short sweet contemporary romances you've read. Some of them have featured touches of the paranormal, but these touches have been lighthearted, whimsical, fun. So, spirits have a place in your target genre, but they're different kinds of spirits.

Can you convert the vengeful spirit into something lighthearted, whimsical and fun? What if your lead opened a shop and, while renovating it, freed the ghost of a sweet, slightly dotty old gentleman, a previous owner of the shop, who fell through the floor 150 years ago? His body was never found, and thinking he had simply wandered off, his family had repaired the floor, trapping his spirit.

That works. Now we have the genre-appropriate crisis:

Suppose a woman renovating an old shop freed the spirit of a kindly old man who once owned it.

2. The Crisis Must Turn Your Lead's Life Upside Down in a Negative Way

A crisis isn't a crisis unless it throws the lead's life into serious disarray. If the crisis isn't "bad" enough, your readers won't believe the lead would make solving it her top priority. Moreover, it won't take the lead long enough—an entire novel's length— to set things right, and your story will run out of steam halfway down the track.

Does our Suppose meet criteria #2? Would freeing the old man's spirit have a major negative effect on our lead's life? Not necessarily. How can we further shape the Suppose so it turns our lead's life upside down in a negative way?

What if the old gentleman is so grateful to our lead for freeing him that he appoints himself her protector—and scares away every man who's interested in her, including one our lead is interested in? That works. Here's our reshaped Suppose.

> Suppose a woman renovating an old shop freed the spirit of a kindly old man who once owned the shop, and who now shows his gratitude by scaring away the woman's potential suitors.

3. The Crisis Must Capture Your Imagination

The situation the crisis creates must intrigue you. You'll be with this novel a long time. If you get bored while you're writing it, you may not finish it. If you're bored and finish it anyway, you can bet agents and editors will share your boredom—and return your manuscript.

Do you really want to run with this idea? If not, identify the aspect or aspects you don't like and change them. In the Suppose we've been shaping, for example, maybe you like the idea of the lead freeing a ghost but find the idea of the ghost being that of the shop's long-ago owner dull. So you do some brainstorming.

What if the ghost were that of a beautiful young woman instead? Perhaps she becomes jealous of the men interested in our lead. This scenario suggests other kinds of situations down the line.

Maybe you like the idea of the ghost being the old man but you don't like him scaring away suitors. What if our lead has a partner in the shop, another woman, but the ghost appears only to our lead—and when he does, it's to instruct her in the "proper" running of the shop? This scenario suggests its own quite different set of situations.

If your Suppose doesn't capture your imagination and you're stumped as to what to do about it, here are some ideas for shaking things up.

Make It Worse. Change the event or situation so its consequences will be more dire.

Suppose a man lost in a hospital happened upon someone dismembering a body.

Make It Bigger. Enlarge an event or situation.

Suppose the director of a wild-animal park arrived at work and discovered all the animals had escaped and were heading for a nearby village.

Change Certain Elements. Alter certain aspects of an event or situation.

Suppose a woman found a killer waiting for her in her hotel room, killed him, and then discovered it was her *husband*.

Change the Locale. Drop an event or situation into a different setting—from city to country, from tenement to townhouse.

Suppose a floor of a posh London hotel were infested with tarantulas.

Combine Two Supposes. Juxtapose part of one story with part of another.

Suppose a woman on her way to her hotel room was taken hostage by a man on a shooting rampage in the corridor.

Once you've reshaped your Suppose, test it against the three crisis criteria, and make any necessary modifications so it fits all three.

Take your time devising a Suppose that works; it's the foundation upon which you'll build your entire novel. A poorly conceived Suppose will cause a story to crumble somewhere along the way. A well-crafted Suppose will give a novel strength and energy right to the end.

THE STORY GOAL

Once you have selected a crisis, you must decide what your lead is going to do about it. Your lead must set a goal that he believes, when achieved, will solve the crisis. This goal is the *story goal*. To work effectively, it must meet four criteria.

1. Possession or Relief

Your lead, in trying to solve the crisis, must be trying to gain:

* possession of something (a person, an object, information—anything) or
* relief from something (fear, pain, sadness, loneliness, domination, oppression—again, anything).

A man whose story goal is to rescue his kidnapped daughter is seeking possession of something: his child. A young woman who resolves to flee a marriage her father has arranged for her is seeking relief from something: her father's domination.

Have your lead set a goal that would solve the crisis—restore her life to normal—by gaining possession of something or relief from something.

Our shopkeeper with the overprotective ghost might set a goal of restoring her life to normal by putting the old man's ghost to rest without hurting him (he is, after all, a dear old thing). This goal falls into the relief category.

2. Terrible Consequences

Your lead must face terrible consequences if she fails to achieve this goal. The lead must have a lot at stake.

If the man fails to rescue his daughter, he'll suffer the loss of his child. If the young woman fails to free herself from her father's domination, she will be trapped in a marriage she doesn't want. Our shopkeeper faces life without love—a terrible consequence—if she can't free herself from the ghost's protective scare tactics.

3. A Worthy Motivation

Your lead must have at least one worthy, high-minded motivation for pursuing this goal. Readers must be able to root for your lead in his mission, to admire his efforts. They will not do so unless they approve of your lead's motivation for seeking his story goal. Examples of worthy, high-minded motivations are

* duty
* love

- honor
- justice
- dignity
- integrity
- patriotism
- redemption
- self-respect

The detective on the trail of a murderer is motivated by justice. The woman who resolves to help her son kick his crack addiction is motivated by love.

Note that softer motivations, such as kindness and generosity, do not work as effectively. Nor do negative motivations, such as lust, envy, anger, covetousness, excessive pride, hatred and greed.

Revenge is also hard to pull off because many readers have trouble sympathizing with a lead whose story goal is to get even with someone. The only instance in which readers feel that a lead is justified in seeking revenge is when the justice system has failed to punish someone who clearly deserves punishment. An example is the movie *Death Wish*, in which the lead takes it on himself to execute his wife's killers.

But I would discourage you from using revenge as your lead's motivation, at least when you're starting out and need as many cards stacked in your favor as possible. A lead acting out of a negative motivation is an antihero, and effective antiheroes are more difficult to create than effective heroes. Novels with antiheroes are also harder to sell to publishers.

Our shopkeeper's motivation in trying to gently rid herself of her ghost is love—both her fondness for the ghost, which motivates her not to hurt him, and her desire to have love in her own life.

4. Tremendous Odds

To achieve the story goal, your lead must be working against tremendous odds. It should appear practically impossible for your lead to achieve her objective.

The Southern police chief who hears a rumor that her senator husband is a member of the Ku Klux Klan faces enormous odds in trying to learn the truth. It's practically impossible to learn the identity of Klan members, and if her husband does belong, it will be especially difficult to unhood a man with so much to protect.

Our shopkeeper will have no easy time laying her spirit to rest. After all, he's been in the shop (or under it) for 150 years.

THE STORY IDEA

If necessary, revise your lead's story goal so it meets all four criteria. Then combine it with your Suppose in the following format:

Suppose _____
_____
_____ .

S/he decides s/he must _____
_____
_____ .

This is your *story idea*, the essence of your novel. But it's probably quite different from the notion you started with. Once again, ask yourself if this concept appeals to you. Can you imagine constructing a story around a lead with this crisis, seeking this goal to solve the crisis?

If the story idea doesn't appeal to you, or if you're unsure, try again. You're just playing with ideas at this stage and have nothing to lose. Keep trying until you have a crisis and a story goal that combine to form a story idea you really like. Then move on to step three, where you'll bring your story idea to life.

To Recap
- Your story idea begins with a crisis for your lead—a Suppose.
- The crisis must be genre-appropriate, it must turn your lead's life upside down in a negative way, and it must capture your imagination.
- Some sources of Supposes are your life, your family, your friends, your co-workers, the media, travel, dreams and eavesdropping.

- Enhance a Suppose by worsening it, enlarging it, altering it, moving it and/or combining it with another Suppose.
- Give your lead a story goal for solving the crisis. Your lead must seek possession or relief, face terrible consequences if he fails, have a worthy motivation, and confront tremendous odds.

Creating Your Lead

In This Step
- The character fact list
- Defining your story's main character

There's an old argument among novelists. Some insist that characters determine plot, while others maintain that plot determines characters. I say both sides are right. Characters' personalities inevitably affect how a story develops. But your story idea helps you define your characters.

DEFINING THE LEAD

Your lead is your novel's most important character, the hero or heroine of your story. Every novel needs a lead; a novel without a lead is like a movie without a star.

To define your lead, as well as your other major characters, use the character fact list—a compilation of the facts you need to know about a character before you begin plotting your story. Use all the following categories every time you create a character fact list.

CHARACTER FACT LIST

Character Type:

Connection to Lead:

Story Goal:

Gender:

Age:

Appearance

Height:

Body Type:

Hair Color:

Eye Color:

Mannerisms:

Distinctive Speech Pattern:

Personality:

Background:

Personal Life:

Private Life:

Work Life:

Strength:

Weakness:

Name:

Let's discuss each item in terms of your lead.

Character Type
This is the role this character plays in your novel (lead, opposition, confidant or romantic involvement). For this character, write "Lead."

Connection to Lead
This is the character's relationship to the lead. Since you are defining the lead, leave this blank.

Story Goal
You defined your lead's story goal in step two. Enter it here.

Gender

Enter what you decided in step two.

Age

Your Suppose may suggest your lead's age. For example, if you had "Suppose a young widow with an infant falls in love with a man who she thinks dislikes children," you might make her in her mid twenties. If you had "Suppose the emperor of a distant planet learned that his subjects would die if they remained on the planet," you might make him somewhere in his thirties or forties so he has some life experience.

Your target genre may suggest the age of your lead. For example, if you're writing a novel for eight- to twelve-year-olds, you know from step two (page 17) that your lead should be twelve, the age of your oldest reader. If you're writing a cozy mystery featuring an older female sleuth, you might make your lead somewhere in her sixties or seventies. If you're writing a legal thriller, you know from reading these novels that they usually feature leads in their thirties.

If you're writing a book for a specific publisher's "line"—for example, one of the romance lines at Harlequin or Silhouette—obtain the publisher's guidelines, or "tip sheet," for writers. (Send a request to the publisher's editorial department, enclosing a self-addressed stamped envelope.) Often the particulars on the tip sheet will include age ranges for the lead.

Appearance

You already know whether your lead is male or female, and you know his or her age. There may be further clues to appearance in your Suppose. Perhaps your lead's ethnic background is integral; for example, you're writing a multicultural romance and have already designated your lead as African-American. If your Suppose is about a male model, he'd have to be good-looking. The lead in a historical novel about a Roman soldier or a sea captain or a medieval nun would have a distinctive appearance.

Your target genre may suggest your lead's appearance. For example, if you're writing a historical romance, you know from reading such novels that your lead must be beautiful.

You may have had a mental picture of your lead all along, simply because it came to you. Perhaps your lead is a seasoned homicide detective in a big city and you've already decided he's a bachelor who doesn't take care of himself. He's overweight, unkempt, gray from too many cigarettes.

Jot down any appearance traits you've come up with using the above means. For example,

Female
Early twenties
African-American
Gorgeous
Voluptuous figure

or

Male
Late fifties
Fat
Pasty
Unkempt

Now you'll use a shortcut used by many veteran novelists. Gather all the magazines and catalogs you can find and, with your notes beside you, look for a color photograph of a person whose appearance fits your notes. When you find one, try to imagine this person as the subject of your novel—in action, interacting with other characters.

When you find someone you like, paste the picture onto a piece of paper or cardboard, leaving a few inches of blank space at the bottom. Often a catalog or magazine will run a number of shots of the same person in different clothes and settings. Cut out all the pictures you can find of this person and create a collage of your lead.

Put this photo sheet on the wall where it will be in constant view. Refer to it as you record the details of your lead's appearance.

Height and Body Type

Tall and willowy? Short and stocky? Muscular? Scrawny? Voluptuous? Sylphlike?

Hair Color

Blond, brown, black (raven), red, auburn, gray, white? Light, medium or dark?

Eye Color

Gray, green, blue, violet, brown, deep brown, hazel?

Mannerisms

Study the photo sheet and use your imagination to picture your lead in action—talking, walking, sitting, eating, laughing. How would you describe his or her manner? Does he gesticulate excitedly when speaking, or is he always controlled and subdued? Does she smile a lot? Frown a lot? Turn her head in sharp, birdlike movements? Or is she languid, never moving quickly for anything or anyone?

Pay particular attention to the eyes. Does he slide shy glances? Open his eyes wide when happy? Does he have trouble meeting people's gaze?

Distinctive Speech Pattern

Again, in your mind: When your lead speaks, what stands out? Does she pepper her sentences with curses? Is she careful in her speech, weighing every word, eager to never offend? Does he make liberal use of hyperbole? Does she tend to downplay everything? Does he often come out with malapropisms? Does she fall back on clichés? Does he use a lot of big words? Does she have a favorite expression; for example, calling all her women friends "doll" or "honey" or "girlfriend"? Is he well spoken? Does she make frequent grammatical mistakes?

Who your lead is will help determine his speech pattern. A professor speaks differently than a prostitute; an adult differently than a child; a twelfth-century monk differently than a twentieth-century gang member.

Personality

It's vital that your reader like your lead. If not, the reader won't care if your lead succeeds or fails in her quest, and a reader who doesn't care stops reading. You can ensure reader sympathy by giving your lead four specific personality traits. They are traits that have been shared by heroes and heroines for as long as people have told each other stories.

1. *Courage*. Your lead should possess an inner strength which will enable her to confront obstacles that arise as she pursues her story goal. This courage needn't be an obvious attribute; your lead may have a quiet or hidden courage, so she sometimes falters before pulling herself up and facing adversity.

2. *Virtue*. Your lead should be a moral person who knows right from wrong, who understands the difference between good and evil. He's no saint—he is human, and humans don't always take the high road—but at the end of the day, if he's done something illegal, immoral or unethical, he knows it and seeks to make reparation.

3. *Likability*. Your lead should have a sense of humor and be able to laugh at herself. She must be modest about her good qualities, though not falsely so. She must be kind, considerate and concerned about the welfare of others.

4. *Competence*. Your lead should be a sensible, intelligent person who makes full use of these qualities when dealing with problems and obstacles. If he can't always be clever, he must at least possess common sense.

Background

What has your lead's life been like up to now? Use any clues in your Suppose, and let your imagination fill in the rest. You needn't go into exhaustive detail; a few paragraphs will suffice. Following are some areas to explore:

- Geography: Where was she born? Where did she grow up? Was she raised in one place, or did her family move around?
- Family: What were his parents like? Does he have siblings? Was he close to any of them? Did he marry? Have any children?
- Childhood: What was his childhood like? Was he happy, well adjusted, popular? Miserable, out of place, lonely? Why?
- Education/Vocation: Did she go to college? If so, where? Did she do graduate work? Did she receive any other kind of training? What is her work history?

Personal Life

Where does she live? In a house, an apartment, a co-op, a condo? In what state, in what city or town (real or made up), on what street?

Who else is at home? Is she married? Does she live with someone she's not married to—a partner, a parent? Are there children? If so, what are their names and ages? Any pets?

What is your lead's social life like? Who are his friends? Who is his best friend? Someone at work? What does he do with his friends? Does she work out at the gym early every morning? Take her son to Cub Scouts every Wednesday night? Enjoy bowling with the girls, bridge with her husband, after-hours dance clubs with her boyfriend, museums on Sunday afternoons?

Private Life

What does your lead do when she's alone? What are her hobbies and interests? Does she like to read, watch TV, listen to music, take walks, paint, write, walk her dog?

Work Life

What does he do for a living? Where does he work, in an office or at home? Does he travel? Who are his co-workers? Whom does he report to? Who reports to him? Who are his allies? His rivals?

Strength

What is your lead's strongest positive trait (in addition to courage, virtue, likability and competence)? Examples are humor, loyalty, fairness, kindness, ingenuity, tolerance, discretion, generosity and adaptability.

Weakness

What is your lead's strongest negative trait, her flaw? Examples are envy, greed, vanity, laziness, arrogance, insecurity, narcissism, intolerance, selfishness, conceitedness and false pride.

Name

Write the character's name here, and write it using a thick marker in the space you left at the bottom of the photo sheet.

A character's name must truly fit or, like a cheap suit, it will never feel right. Here are some guidelines for naming characters.

Gather source materials. Buy the most comprehensive baby name book you can find for ideas. You can even use a name book just for writers: *The Writer's Digest Character Naming Sourcebook*, by Sherrilyn Kenyon with Hal Blythe and Charlie Sweet (Writer's Digest Books), lists thousands of names from many cultures. Other sources are newspapers, magazines and the telephone book.

Take cues from the character's background. A well-heeled New York attorney might be named Roger or Elliott or Arthur. But those names wouldn't suit a Cuban drug lord working out of Miami, who might be called Jesus or Roberto or Jaime.

Consider whether the character's parents would have selected a certain kind of name. A classics professor might name his daughter Athena. A movie fan in the forties might have named her daughter Ava or Rita.

Make sure a name you're considering was in fashion when the character was born. A man born in 1929 might be named Sidney, but a young boy today probably wouldn't—he might be named Justin. A young girl born today might be named Ashley, but a woman born in the thirties probably wouldn't—she might be named Jean.

Select a name that fits the character's personality. Is he or she a formal sort of person, or more informal? A repressed spinster teacher in an exclusive girls' prep school might be named Diane, but probably not DeeDee—though one of her students might go by that name.

Consider whether your character might have changed her given name to better suit her personality. She might have chosen a nickname, a middle name or a made-up name. For example, a flamboyant young woman trying to break into films might have been christened Katherine Frances Freemont by her conservative Midwestern parents, but when she goes on auditions, she's Franki Freemont.

Use a different first initial for all of your more important characters' first and last names. Readers get confused when there's an Adam and an Alec, a Mrs. Wilson and a Mrs. Webster.

To keep track, write out the alphabet and write down names as you decide on them.

Avoid names that end alike or similarly. Examples are Gloria and Maria, Tony and Bobby, Eileen and Marlene, Bill and Will, Jackson and Robertson.

Vary name lengths and sounds. Not all of your characters should have Anglo names.

Avoid using names ending in s. These make for awkward possessives which trip readers: Thomas's, Lucas's, the Maciases'.

A Sample Lead's Character Fact List

Here's the character fact list as it might look for the lead of a story idea that began as a Suppose in step two (the target genre is thriller).

> Suppose a Southern police chief heard a rumor that her senator husband was a member of the Ku Klux Klan.
>
> She decides she must find out if her husband is a member of the KKK.

CHARACTER FACT LIST

Character Type:	Lead
Connection to Lead:	
Story Goal:	To find out if her husband is a Klan member
Gender:	Female
Age:	36
Appearance	
Height:	5'7"
Body Type:	Thin, wiry, athletic
Hair Color:	Brown

Eye Color:	Pale green
Mannerisms:	Face shows a lot of emotion
Distinctive Speech Pattern:	Controlled, educated way of speaking
Personality:	Courageous, virtuous, likable, competent
Background:	Raised in Boston, only child of affluent parents. Both parents alive in Boston, not part of her life now because they disapprove of her career and have shut her out. Married at twenty-two to a man she met at Boston University; he was abusive and they divorced bitterly a year later; no children. She switched from law to law enforcement, followed a man to Otisville (near New Orleans), later broke up with him, but stayed in Otisville and has worked her way up to chief of police. Four years ago she began dating [name?], a Louisiana senator. After a year they married.
Personal Life:	She and her husband live in a magnificent restored mansion that she insists is too big for two people and too ostentatious for a police chief. He claims it suits a senator perfectly. They have no children, though she wants a baby desperately. She has a fluffy white toy poodle named Pierre. There is a housekeeper, [name?]. Socially, they are active, attending various official functions. They are considered a golden couple. He entertains a lot of his political contacts. She sees [first lieutenant] socially when she can find time. She also

enjoys the company of a neighbor, a
fellow Yankee, who is married to a local
bank president. Lately she finds her
husband increasingly private and
wonders about their future, though she
loves him deeply.

Private Life: Her secret passion is sketching the
wonderful old buildings of the French
Quarter. Sometimes she puts on jeans
and a sweatshirt and wanders around
sketching. She also volunteers at
Helping Hand, a children's shelter.

Work Life: Chief of police in Otisville. For the most
part she has earned the respect of the
officers on her force, though
occasionally conflicts arise because she
is (1) a woman and (2) a Yankee. Her
closest ally is her first lieutenant,
[name?], who has become her close
friend. The atmosphere in the outdated
old building that houses the police
department is friendly but professional.
Since she married the senator, she feels
a difference in the air, a distance from
her officers.

Strength: Gentle kindness toward the weak and
helpless

Weakness: She's got a chip on her shoulder about
being a woman in a man's job; this makes
her defensive, sometimes combative.

Name: Sara Bradford

You now know enough about your lead to begin taking her
through your story. Before you do, though, you must define the
rest of your novel's characters. You'll do that in step four.

To Recap

- Create a character fact list for your lead.
- Your Suppose will provide clues to your lead's appearance, background and characteristics.
- Your lead *must* be courageous, virtuous, likable and competent.

Defining Your Other Characters

In This Step
- The opposition
- The confidant
- The romantic involvement
- Additional characters

Certain character types recur in novels because they play such important roles in the development of the story. In this step you'll define these characters for your novel. The first is the opposition, a must for every novel. The second is the confidant—not a must for every novel, but a must in the Marshall Plan. Finally, there is the romantic involvement; whether you include this character type will depend on your target genre and story idea.

DEFINING THE OPPOSITION

The opposition is the character who *most* stands in the way of the lead's achieving the story goal. Though the opposition is sometimes called the villain, he needn't be evil. He simply has a goal in direct conflict with that of the lead.

The opposition must be a person. It may not be a force of nature, such as a fire, drought, blizzard or earthquake; a group, such as a gang or corporation; or a general life condition, such as poverty, corruption or society's apathy.

The opposition must be an equal match to your lead, a person of roughly similar strengths and abilities, to ensure a good "fight."

The most effective opposition is a character who already plays some part in the lead's life; for example, a husband, a wife, a boss or a business rival. The opposition may have some other connection to the lead; they may have a mutual acquaintance or some shared event in their past.

In some novels the identity of the opposition is not disclosed to the reader until the end, though the opposition's actions are always evident. Examples are a murder mystery or a woman-in-jeopardy suspense novel. In these the opposition is likely to be a character we know; we're just not aware she's the opposition.

The key to devising an effective opposition is to create a character whose motivation for standing in the lead's way is as strong and logical as the lead's motivation to attain his goal. The opposition needn't be working from a negative motivation; indeed, often if the tables were turned, the opposition could be the lead. Take, for example, a Western historical novel in which the lead raises sheep and the opposition raises cattle. Though the opposition's goal is in direct conflict with the lead's, the opposition is not necessarily bad or evil, and a novel could be written in which the two roles were reversed.

A common pitfall I find in novels submitted to me is the opposition who exists solely to obstruct the lead; the opposition has no motivating goal of his own. This kind of opposition runs the risk of turning into an unrealistic, mustache-twirling Snidely Whiplash type of villain. In real life, an opposition is a real person who believes as strongly as the lead does that his motivations are valid and his actions justified.

In *Sleeping With the Enemy*, Nancy Price created an especially effective opposition in Martin, the cruelly abusive husband who loves his wife, Sara, so passionately that when she runs away, he wants to track her down and kill her rather than let her go. His desire for vengeance is largely the product of madness, yet to the end he rationally (at least to *him*) maintains, "They want it," referring to women and abuse.

In *Eye of the Needle*, Ken Follett gave us Henry Faber, the master German spy who tries to use the vulnerable Englishwoman Lucy Rose as his means of escape from the English forces on his trail. He is ruthless in his efforts to win the war for the Nazis, as convinced of the rightness of his cause as any Englishman.

In *The Prime of Miss Jean Brodie*, Muriel Spark gave us Miss Mackay, headmistress of Marcia Blaine School for Girls, who in her conventional dedication to her students proves a potent opposition to the unorthodox, freethinking and equally dedicated Miss Brodie.

Finding Your Lead's Opposition

Who is your lead's opposition? The answer may lie in your Suppose. Here are some Supposes and the oppositions they suggest.

Suppose a visitor to a large hospital happened upon the lair of a twisted murderer working from inside the hospital itself.
   Opposition: the murderer

Suppose a woman discovered that her husband was having an affair with his young secretary.
   Opposition: the secretary?
                the husband?

Suppose a rancher returned home to discover that his wife had been abducted by Indians.
   Opposition: the Indians who abducted her

Suppose a teenage girl received an anonymous threatening letter.
   Opposition: the person who sent the letter

If your Suppose doesn't suggest an opposition, consider your lead's story goal and then list characters who might oppose him and why. Choose the one that seems to have the strongest story potential, then create a character fact list for that character.

Consider Sara Bradford, whose goal is to find out if her husband is a Klan member. Who might be her opposition? Her husband? Perhaps, but not necessarily. Even if he is a Klan member, he may love Sara and not want her to come to harm. Perhaps one of his advisors wants to keep Sara from learning the truth, because the advisor has goals of his own that depend on the senator's remaining a senator. The advisor's goal, then, is to thwart Sara's truth-seeking efforts. Or maybe the opposition is a vicious Klan leader who can't afford to have any of his disciples exposed.

A Sample Opposition's Character Fact List

Here's the character fact list as it might look for Sara's opposition.

CHARACTER FACT LIST

Character Type:	Opposition
Connection to Lead:	Closest advisor to Sara's husband
Story Goal:	To prevent Sara from learning that her husband is a member of the KKK
Gender:	Male
Age:	44
Appearance	
Height:	6'
Body Type:	Muscular build
Hair Color:	Dark blond
Eye Color:	Pale blue
Mannerisms:	Every movement careful and controlled
Distinctive Speech Pattern:	In professional and social situations he affects a smooth, refined way of speaking. When he's off guard, he is vulgar and foulmouthed.
Personality:	Loyal to Sara's husband, but ultimately loyal to himself; ruthless in going after what he wants
Background:	Like Sara, he's a Northerner, but he

experienced nothing of her privileged upbringing. The son of a poor Boston Irish railroad worker, he is the only one of six children who rose out of the squalor. He cut off all ties to his embarrassing roots as soon as he could and changed his name. He worked his way through college, relying on his cunning and good looks to get ahead. Also like Sara, he went to law school, then entered politics and is now the senator's private counsel and advisor.

Personal Life: He's single. He has no time for relationships or a social life, except when he seeks out a certain prostitute who is willing to indulge his violent sexual proclivities.

Private Life: He works out and plays racquetball at the same club as the senator and their high-level colleagues. He sees the club as an opportunity to learn secrets and forge strategic friendships.

Work Life: He works closely with the senator. His friends and enemies are the senator's friends and enemies.

Strength: He never gives up in pursuit of his goal. He is tireless, undauntable.

Weakness: He underestimates the cleverness and intelligence of others.

Name: Allen Gardner (born Leary)

DEFINING THE CONFIDANT

Not every novel has a confidant, but I've made this character a requirement in the Marshall Plan because it adds so much to a story. The confidant is a person close to the lead who is privy to the lead's thoughts, secrets and fears. The confidant can be a friend, a spouse, a lover, a relative, a co-worker, an employee. This character acts as a sounding board, helping the lead make plans, analyze situations and work through problems and dilemmas. The confidant can supply information to the lead, advise her, cajole her, soothe, persuade or confront her. With the confidant, the lead can talk things out naturally. The confidant's story goal is always to help the lead achieve *her* goal.

A writer who provides no confidant for the lead makes her own life more difficult because most of the time, when the lead is working out a problem or deciding on a course of action, he'll have no one to talk things out with. This process must therefore take the form of long passages of introspection, and these can become dull or lifeless. A conversation or argument with another character is far more interesting and dynamic.

Additionally, while the lead and confidant are working out the lead's problems, aspects of the lead's personality come out, helping to characterize her. Think of Watson to Holmes, Hastings to Poirot (you'll find that detectives always make liberal use of the confidant for figuring out their cases), Rhoda Morgenstern to Mary Richards. Even as he or she listens and reacts, the confidant draws out the lead as a human being.

A common error of beginning writers is to create the confidant without subtlety: This character clearly exists only to act as a sounding board for the lead, and whenever the lead has a problem, the confidant practically falls in the door, ready to listen and react. The best kind of confidant is a character who is already part of the lead's life and would naturally play this role, but who has reason to exist in her own right.

For example, in *Jaws*, Peter Benchley makes expert use of Martin Brody's wife, Ellen, as his confidant. Amidst talk of Ellen's recently acquired habit of taking sleeping pills, Brody's haphazard eating habits, and the possibility of tennis lessons for their boys, they discuss the problem of the shark:

"Have you made any progress?"

"You mean about catching that damn thing? No. Meadows called that oceanographer friend of his down

from Woods Hole, so he's here. Not that I see what good
he's going to do."

"What's he like?"

"He's all right, I guess. He's young, a decent-looking guy.
He's a bit of a know-it-all, but that's not surprising. He
seems to know the area pretty well."

"Oh? How so?"

"He said he was a summer kid in Southampton. Spent
all his summers there."

"Working?"

"I don't know, living with his parents probably. He looks
to be the type."

"What type?"

"Rich. Good family. The Southampton summer type. You
ought to know it, for God's sake."

"Don't get angry. I was just asking."

"I'm not angry. I just said you ought to know the type,
that's all. I mean, you're the type yourself."

It's perfectly natural that Brody's wife would ask him how
things are going. And just as naturally he tells her (and the
reader) how he feels about Matt Hooper. Benchley also characterizes Brody in this exchange: We sense that he feels socially
inferior to people of privilege like Matt, and that Brody married
above himself when he married Ellen.

One of the best-loved confidants in literature is Mammy in
Margaret Mitchell's *Gone With the Wind*. Mammy's intimate
role in Scarlett's life makes her a natural sounding board and
advisor, and advise she does—on everything from eating before
the barbecue at Twelve Oaks to Scarlett's breaking her engage-
ment to Rhett Butler, "a mule in hawse harness, jes' lak you."
But, her disapproval notwithstanding, Mammy promises that,
even if Scarlett marries Rhett, "Ah ain' leavin' you. Ah gwine
stay right hyah an' see dis ting thoo." What a confidant—loyal
to the end, her devotion unconditional, her story goal to help
Scarlett achieve *her* story goal of keeping Tara and finding love.

Mitchell wrote of Mammy: ". . . Her code of conduct and her
sense of pride were as high as or higher than those of her

owncrs." We see evidence of these qualities again and again as Mammy voices her disapproval of her scheming charge's behavior. Mammy represents society's disapproval in general, and Scarlett's reactions to this disapproval characterize her beautifully.

Who is your lead's confidant? Reread your lead's character fact list, looking for likely candidates. Could a spouse, a friend, a colleague or an associate play this role more effectively than anyone else? Consider each possible character carefully, and when you've decided on your lead's confidant, create a character fact list for this character.

A Sample Confidant's Character Fact List

Sara Bradford's character fact list, under Work Life, says: "Her closest ally is her first lieutenant, [name?], who has become her close friend." This character would make an excellent confidant for Sara. Here's how the character fact list might look.

CHARACTER FACT LIST

Character Type:	Confidant
Connection to Lead:	Sara's first lieutenant
Story Goal:	To hclp Sara find out if her husband is a member of the KKK
Gender:	Female
Age:	33
Appearance	
Height:	5′3″
Body Type:	Chubby, cuddly
Hair Color:	Auburn
Eye Color:	Brown
Mannerisms:	Exaggerated, comical

Distinctive Speech Pattern:	Heavy Southern accent; uses "darlin'," "sugar" and "sweetie" liberally
Personality:	Mischievous, fun-loving, self-deprecating; jokes about her weight problem
Background:	A local girl, from an honest working-class family, who made good
Personal Life:	Single; she dates the same guy (a loser she's fond of) on and off. She shares her shabbily comfortable apartment with a grouchy old Siamese cat named Custard.
Private Life:	She loves nothing more than to curl up with a romance novel and a bag of potato chips.
Work Life:	Works closely with Sara in the department; her right-hand person
Strength:	Her wonderful sense of humor; her ability to laugh at herself
Weakness:	Out of her insecurity she has built up unrealistically high standards in men—standards that keep her lonely most of the time.
Name:	Rosie Pike

DEFINING THE ROMANTIC INVOLVEMENT

The romantic involvement is a character who is the object of your lead's romantic and/or sexual interest. The romantic involvement's story goal is always to win, or keep, the lead's love.

Not every novel should have a romantic involvement. Whether to include one depends on the kind of novel you're writing.

You'll know from your reading if novels in your target genre usually include a romantic involvement. Any sort of romance, obviously, has a romantic involvement. In many suspense novels the lead is involved in a romantic relationship while pursuing the story goal. In novels of romantic suspense, there is, of course, always a romantic involvement. In other kinds of novels—mysteries, for instance—a romantic involvement is optional.

If your target genre requires a romantic involvement, you'll have to create this character.

If a romantic involvement is optional for the kind of novel you're writing, you must decide whether to include a character who plays this role.

Aspects of Love

First consider your lead's circumstances, like whether your lead is already involved in a committed romantic relationship. This does not mean such a relationship makes a romantic involvement out of the question; it just gives the situation a whole new dynamic. If your lead is married or living with someone or committed to someone, she can still have a new romantic relationship, but keep in mind that in the Marshall Plan, the lead and the romantic involvement always end up together. That means you'll be ending the old relationship. Is your lead in an unhappy marriage? Living with someone she doesn't really love? Stuck in a relationship that's going nowhere? These are all situations in which a new romantic relationship could work.

If your lead isn't involved in any sort of committed relationship, consider what effect a romantic relationship could have on his life. Is he lonely? Often the lead's achievement of the story goal is made far richer because the lead has found someone with whom to share his restored happiness.

Consider also that the ups and downs, aparts and togethers of a developing romantic relationship can add a nice layer of tension to the lead's life as she pursues her story goal. And anything that adds to the lead's state of uneasiness, that increases her state of anxiety and doubt, is good in terms of storytelling. Think of the harried detective who arrives home so exhausted she can barely eat dinner, but who has a date with the romantic involvement that night. You can bet on conflict as her job gets in the way of their relationship. Consider the firefighter whose wife begs him to give up his dangerous work for the sake of her and of their children. The romantic involvement (the wife) causes him to feel tension and anxiety both at work and at home—also good for your story.

In *Sins*, by Judith Gould, fashion-magazine queen Hélène Junot schemes to avenge the sins that have been committed against her and her family. At the same time she tries again and again to make a permanent connection with the great love of her life, Nigel Somerset. Her inability to do so adds frustration and loneliness to her life as she pursues her story goal. At the end of the novel, Hélène and Nigel narrowly escape death at the hands of an assassin. Hélène finds herself praying, to a God she thought she didn't believe in, for Nigel to live. When it's clear he will live, she finds also that she no longer desires her long-sought revenge because now, with Nigel here to love her, that revenge no longer matters.

> A sob caught in her throat. For a long moment she was silent. "*. . . And . . . and forgive us our trespasses*," she said in a fervent whisper, "*as we forgive those who trespass against us*."

In this case, the lead's fulfillment at winning the romantic involvement is so great that she doesn't relish achieving the story goal; she is now able to see, through the contentment love brings, that her goal is no longer important, and she lets it go. It's an extremely effective device if used judiciously. If you use it, make sure your lead *believes* she must achieve her story goal right up to the moment she releases it.

Would a romantic involvement add to the texture and complexity of your novel? If the answer is yes, you should probably have one. Looking for likely candidates, reread your story idea and your lead's character fact list. Think about how this character might come into your lead's life or already be a part of it, then create a character fact list for the romantic involvement.

A Sample Romantic Involvement's Character Fact List

Rereading Sara Bradford's story idea and character fact list, it seems to me a romantic involvement could add an interesting dimension to her story. As she begins to see her husband in a new light and begins to realize he's not the man she thought she married, she can become open to a new romantic relationship, one that will have no lies or deception. I'll use these ideas to create Sara's romantic interest—Eric Montero, one of her officers, who has had enough of deceitful relationships and believes he can have something honest and good with Sara. Here's how his character fact list might look.

CHARACTER FACT LIST

Character Type:	Romantic involvement
Connection to Lead:	He's an officer on Sara's force.
Story Goal:	To win Sara's love
Gender:	Male
Age:	33
Appearance	
Height:	5'10"
Body Type:	Stocky, solid muscle
Hair Color:	Black
Eye Color:	Black
Mannerisms:	Easy gait, relaxed manner, but lightning reflexes in a tense situation
Distinctive Speech Pattern:	Faint Hispanic accent
Personality:	Sexy, macho, fair minded
Background:	Of Colombian descent; grew up in New Orleans
Personal Life:	His mother lives with him and takes care of his daughter.

Private Life:	Nearly every night he has gone out to drink and meet women—until the possibility of a relationship with Sara arose.
Work Life:	He reports to Sara; there has always been a tension, an electricity, between them.
Strength:	A big, warm, generous heart; hopelessly romantic and sentimental
Weakness:	Macho defensiveness, a remnant of a rough youth
Name:	Eric Montero

DEFINING YOUR OTHER CHARACTERS

Your novel will include numerous other characters who will not play "official" roles. Some of the characters will be important to your story; others, not as important—perhaps just names from characters' pasts. You'll find you've already created most, if not all, of these characters in your character fact lists. Reread them, looking for characters you've mentioned or suggested, some of whom you may not even have named. Name them now, then list them, leaving space under each name for notes. You'll undoubtedly add to this list as your novel progresses.

Here's my list from Sara's story.

Kirk Layton: Sara's ex-husband
Ian Thomas: Sara's lover after her divorce
Lance Bradford: Sara's husband, the senator
Connie Farnsworth: Lance's administrative assistant
Juanita Nuñez: the Bradfords' housekeeper
Helen Davidson: the Bradfords' neighbor; Sara's fellow
    Yankee
Vicki Yost: head of Helping Hand, the children's shelter where
    Sara volunteers
Xaviera: Allen Gardner's prostitute friend
Ollie Zack: Rosie's sometime boyfriend

"Queenie" Montero: Eric's mother
Wanda Montero: Eric's daughter
Ursula: Eric's ex-wife

Keep your list of additional characters with your character fact lists on your desk for easy reference. In step five, you'll put these characters in action.

To Recap
- Designate the opposition and create a character fact list.
- Designate the confidant and create a character fact list.
- Decide whether your novel should have a romantic involvement; if it should, designate this character and create a character fact list.
- Reread your character fact lists for additional characters. List each new one with a brief descriptive tag.

Part 2

YOUR COMPLETE GUIDE TO PLOTTING

In This Part . . .

This part shows you how to plot your novel.

Getting Off to the Right Start

In This Step
- Classic novel structure
- Story length
- Sections
- Section sheets
- Plotting your first sections

OK, you have your target genre, a story idea and some characters. Why not just start writing? Because without some kind of plan, a map of the route your story will take, you're practically guaranteed to start with a bang and, sooner or later, look up and say, "Now what?" To push the metaphor a little further, you'll have a full tank of gas, but you'll be at a crossroads and have no idea which road to take. You won't know where you're going!

Anyone can write a great beginning. Show me an unpublished novelist, and I'll show you a drawer full of false starts. The trick is to keep your story running without stalling or blocking. To achieve this end, you must have, at the very least, a basic notion of the course your lead will take to achieve her story goal. That's where plotting comes in.

THE CLASSIC STRUCTURE

Before you can begin plotting, you must understand the basic structure of the novel. It's a classic form, defined first by Aristotle in *Poetics*, and for our purposes it's enough to know

Beginning
Middle
End

that it consists of three parts: the beginning, the middle and the end.

The beginning constitutes the first quarter of your novel. Here you'll set up your story situation, introduce all your characters, present all necessary background information and, most importantly, begin all of your story lines: your lead's main story line—in pursuit of the story goal—and any other subplots you decide to include.

The middle constitutes half your novel's length. It contains the principal action of the lead's story line and all the subplots, as well as twists and surprises and complications.

The end constitutes your novel's last quarter. Here all story lines resolve themselves, most notably your lead's main story line, which moves through distinct phases as it builds to the climactic moment and then, finally, wraps itself up.

Note that these divisions should not be visible to the reader. They exist solely to help you structure your story.

In this step, you'll start plotting your novel's beginning. Before you can do that, however, you must ascertain the correct length for your novel as a whole.

DETERMINING YOUR NOVEL'S IDEAL LENGTH

Any given type of novel has a customary length or length range. The flexibility of this length requirement depends on the kind of book. Traditionally, book lengths have been expressed in terms of the approximate number of words the book contains. For example, at this writing, a novel in Silhouette Books' romance line must run from 53,000 to 58,000 words. A novel in Silhouette's Special Edition line must run from 75,000 to 80,000 words. These are relatively tight ranges, when you consider that 1,000 words equal only four manuscript pages. On the other hand, a historical romance for Avon Books may run from 100,000 to 125,000 words, a looser range.

Why should you even worry about manuscript length? Why can't you just write your book and let it end where it wants to? First and most important, because publishers require these lengths. They have several reasons for doing so. On a purely business level, manufacturing costs require that a book fall within a certain length range in order to be profitable. In the case of paperbacks, books must meet length requirements that allow a predetermined number of books to fit into a bookstore shelf pocket; even before that, a certain number of books must fit in a shipping carton. This mechanization of art may sound crass, but it's how publishing works—a reality we have to work with if we want to sell novels.

A less hard-nosed reason is that readers have come to expect that certain kinds of books will run to certain lengths. Fans of Silhouette Romances don't want books stretched to a leisurely 100,000 words any more than devotees of Avon historical romances want books that weigh in at a puny 53,000 words.

How do you find the correct word length for the novel you're writing? You can use several methods.

Check with the publishers of your kind of book to see if they offer tip sheets. These will state a length requirement.

Another way to find length requirement is to consult how-to writing books devoted to your genre; you'll find these books in your bookstore or library. For example, if you're writing a mystery, you can refer to *How to Write Mysteries*, by Shannon OCork (Writer's Digest Books). On page 9 you'll find: "The average mystery novel is 60,000-65,000 words. . . ." If you're writing a romance, you can check out *How to Write a Romance and Get It Published*, by Kathryn Falk (Signet). Here, in chapter one, "Introduction to Category Romances," you'll find word lengths for all types of romance novels.

If you're writing a category novel for a specific publisher's program and can't find the word length by any of the above methods, call the publisher's editorial department and ask an editorial assistant what the preferred word length is for novels in the program.

Failing all of this, you can come up with an approximate word count on your own by taking a book of the type you're writing and applying the following formula:

Book pages × lines on a full page × 9 = number of words

Do this for half a dozen books like yours and then average their word counts.

SECTIONS AND SECTION SHEETS

You now know the correct word length for your novel, but before you start plotting, let me introduce the device that will serve as your plotting tool: the *section sheet*.

A section sheet is a template on which you will plan a single unit of action in your novel—a *section*. Presently we'll go into more specifics about what happens in a section and how to record those events on a section sheet. For now, though, you must assemble the correct number of section sheets for your novel. To do this, refer to the NovelMaster in Figure 1.

Round the word length you just came up with to the nearest thousand, and find this rounded number in one of the word-length ranges in the far left column. Read across to the number in the "Number of Sections" column headed "Total." This is how many section sheets you'll need for your entire novel.

To illustrate this step, let's use Sara's story. We've already determined this novel will be a thriller. Since a thriller is not a category type of novel, no publishers offer a tip sheet that would state an appropriate word length. Nor is there a how-to guide to refer to. So I've taken six thrillers of the type I have in mind, applied the formula and averaged the word lengths to come up with 120,444 words. When we round this figure to the nearest thousand, we get 120,000 words. I find this number in the 120,000–124,000 word range and read across to the "Number of Sections" column headed "Total," where I find 96—the number of section sheets Sara's story will require.

Figure 2 is a blank section sheet. Photocopy it to get the number of copies you need.

THE NOVELMASTER

Word Length	Number of Sections				VP Characters	Distribution of Sections for Entire Novel					
	Beg.	Mid.	End	Total		Lead	VP #2	VP #3	VP #4	VP #5	VP #6
50,000-54,000	10	20	10	40	2	24	16				
55,000-59,000	11	22	11	44	2	26	18				
60,000-64,000	12	24	12	48	2	29	19				
65,000-69,000	13	26	13	52	3	31	11	10			
70,000-74,000	14	28	14	56	3	34	11	11			
75,000-79,000	15	30	15	60	3	36	12	12			
80,000-84,000	16	32	16	64	3	38	13	13			
85,000-89,000	17	34	17	68	3	41	14	13			
90,000-94,000	18	36	18	72	4	43	10	10	9		
95,000-99,000	19	38	19	76	4	46	11	10	9		
100,000-104,000	20	40	20	80	4	48	11	11	10		
105,000-109,000	21	42	21	84	4	50	12	11	11		
110,000-114,000	22	44	22	88	4	53	12	12	11		
115,000-119,000	23	46	23	92	5	55	10	9	9	9	
120,000-124,000	24	48	24	96	5	58	10	10	9	9	
125,000-129,000	25	50	25	100	5	60	10	10	10	10	
130,000-134,000	26	52	26	104	5	62	11	11	10	10	
135,000-139,000	27	54	27	108	5	65	11	11	11	10	
140,000-144,000	28	56	28	112	6	67	9	9	9	9	9
145,000-149,000	29	58	29	116	6	70	10	9	9	9	9
150,000-154,000	30	60	30	120	6	72	10	10	10	10	9

Figure 1

THE SECTION SHEET

Action	FROM # # SECTION CHARACTER:	Reaction
	Where:	
	When:	
Goal From Character's Last Section		Failure From Character's Last Action Section
Against		With
Conflict		Emotional
		Rational
Failure (Unless Opposition)		
New Goal (OR Go to a Reaction Section)		New Goal

TO #

Figure 2

Number your section sheets consecutively, placing the number next to the large # at the top.

We're concentrating on your novel's beginning now. Refer again to the NovelMaster in Figure 1. On the line for your word-length range, read across to the "Number of Sections" column headed "Beginning." This is the number of section sheets your novel's beginning will contain. Take this number of sheets from the pile you just numbered and set aside the rest for now.

As stated earlier, a section is a unit of story action in a novel. Sections interlock in a chain of action/reaction that is the essence of plotting. Each section is planned on a section sheet. Later, when you actually write your novel, you'll write from your section sheets.

A section may be either of two types: an *action* section or a *reaction* section.

THE ACTION SECTION

An action section is a unit of story in which the *section character* attempts to achieve a short-term *section goal* that he thinks will help him overcome an obstacle he faces and take him closer to achieving his story goal. Usually this attempt involves another character who also appears in the section and who has reason to oppose the section character's efforts (other characters may, of course, be present).

Let's take as an example a novel in which a pair of criminals running from the police have forced themselves into a woman's home and are holding her and her invalid father hostage. The woman's story goal is to get her and her father out of the house and away from their captors. An example of a section goal would be to slip a note requesting rescue out the window when the men aren't looking.

In the course of trying to achieve the section goal, the section character meets resistance through some type of conflict with another character. This conflict can be talking, arguing, fighting, wheedling, seducing, chasing, waiting, searching, fleeing, manipulating, cajoling, insisting, demanding or anything else that puts the characters in opposition regarding the section goal. At the end of this struggle/encounter, the section character experiences a *failure* in one of three forms:

- He fails to achieve the section goal.
- He not only fails to achieve the section goal, but he also learns of a new, even larger problem or obstacle that makes matters even worse.
- He achieves the section goal but learns of a new, even larger problem or obstacle than the one he has just overcome.

The failure must be a natural consequence of the section character's efforts. It may *not* take the form of some external problem unrelated to the conflict. For example, if during the conflict phase, your section character is quarreling with his neighbor, the failure cannot come in the form of a sudden storm that drives your section character inside. The failure must relate to the quarrel.

The failure must never involve coincidence. We've all experienced coincidence in real life, but readers find coincidence in fiction contrived. If during the conflict phase, the section character is running from the opposition who for some reason is trying to kill her, the failure cannot be that she hides in an empty house and discovers that it belongs to the opposition.

The section ends with this failure. In most cases you'll go next to another action section, in which the section character pursues a new section goal he devised as a result of the failure. This new short-term goal, he believes, will help him overcome this new obstacle and, in turn, take him closer to achieving his story goal.

If the failure was especially devastating, you'll go to a reaction section, in which you'll show the section character reacting to the failure and devising his new section goal.

Sometimes an action section will have no visible opposing character—for example, the section character may be alone and searching for something, running from someone whose identity he doesn't know, or performing any kind of activity he thinks will help him attain his section goal but doesn't involve direct interaction with another character. All novels have sections like these, and you should include them when they make sense in your story.

THE REACTION SECTION

A reaction section is a unit of story action in which the section character reacts to the failure she experienced in the preceding action section. The section character may be alone or with another character, most commonly the confidant. If the section character is alone, her reaction is shown through her thoughts and actions. If she is with another character, her reaction is shown primarily through dialogue, though it can be shown through thoughts and actions as well.

The first phase of the reaction section is the emotional phase, in which the section character could be said to respond with her heart to the failure. She feels angry, outraged, insulted, frustrated, embarrassed, or whatever emotion would be natural in the situation.

After reacting emotionally, the section character pulls herself together, cools down and is able to react with her head—rationally.

In the rational phase of the reaction section, you first show the section character trying to analyze the failure and understand exactly what transpired. Then you show her trying to decide what action to take to solve the new problem brought about by the failure.

Finally she settles on a new course of action, setting a new short-term goal—the goal of the next section, an action section. A reaction section is always followed by an action section.

WHEN TO USE A REACTION SECTION

When you're completing an action section sheet, stop after you describe the character's failure and consider what his emotional reaction will be. If it will clearly be strong—the character will be extremely upset or disappointed or devastated or furious, for example—you need a reaction section to show this emotion.

You also need a reaction section if the character's rational response—either analysis or option weighing—will necessarily be complex or extended.

To use a general rule of thumb: The more devastating or momentous the failure in the action section, the likelier it is you'll need a reaction section.

USING THE SECTION SHEET

The section sheet is a template on which you plan the action of a section.

To use it as an action section sheet, fold back the page on the right vertical line and either staple or tape the flap in place. To use it as a reaction section sheet, fold back the page on the left vertical line. You'll now have the correct headings for the section you're planning.

Throughout most of the plotting process, you'll be free to plan your action and reaction sections as you see fit. However, certain sections have special requirements. These sections follow.

SECTION SHEET #1

Section #1 is an action section (fold down the right-hand flap) about your lead (enter her name as the section character). It ends with her first failure—the crisis you've already devised—which will cause your lead to set the story goal, triggering the story itself.

Goal From Character's Last Section

There's no last section, of course, since this is the first, so leave this area blank. At the beginning of a novel, before the crisis hits, the lead does, however, have an implicit goal: to continue living his life according to the status quo. Therefore, in section #1 you want to show your lead in a setting that is typical of his generally happy, precrisis, day-to-day life.

Think about your lead's crisis. What might he be doing when this crisis occurs? Where would he be? What time of day would it be? Exactly how would the crisis occur? Once you have decided these points, fill in "Where" and "When" on the section sheet. (For example, "Monday morning," "At the office.") Then, in the "Conflict" area, describe what your lead is doing just before the crisis hits. For example:

1. Billi is teaching her freshman biology class . . .

2. Laura has just arrived home from work and is waiting for Timmy's school bus . . .

3. David is in his office, arguing with a disgruntled client on the phone . . .

4. Victoria is napping in her stateroom . . .

Have your lead engaged in behavior that is typical of her everyday life—depending, of course, on where your lead is likely to be when the crisis occurs. For ideas about what to have your lead doing, review Work Life, Personal Life and Private Life on her character fact list.

Against

In section #1, "Against" refers to the person or circumstance that brings about the crisis itself. For instance, a letter containing shocking news could arrive, someone could call or ask to speak to the lead, or the lead could learn something or happen upon something or someone. Examples:

1. . . . when the principal appears at the door, motioning for Billi to come out.
   Against: The principal's news

2. . . . when Peter arrives home from work early.
   Against: Peter

3. . . . when his secretary drops a letter marked "Personal" in his inbox.
   Against: What's in the letter

4. . . . when Aunt Cora rushes in, gasping for breath.
   Against: What's upsetting Aunt Cora

Conflict

In section #1, "Conflict" refers to the occurrence of the crisis, and then to any behavior on your lead's part that constitutes shock, disbelief, denial, devastation, surprise, anger, amazement—any feelings your lead would likely have in response to the crisis. For instance:

1.

Gently, the principal tells Billi that her son, Stephen, has just been killed during a robbery in a convenience store. The police are here to talk to her. Billi, in shock, laughs and says that's impossible; Stephen is at home, waiting for her; they have a reservation for dinner to celebrate his nineteenth birthday.

2.

Peter says he's been doing a lot of thinking since his fortieth birthday. He's decided he's not happy in his life, in his marriage. He's divorcing Laura, and he intends to get full custody of Timmy. Furious, Laura slaps him, tells him she's not some servant he can dismiss. What about their years together, working to build their life? Peter says he wants no part of it anymore; it's meaningless because he doesn't love Laura and realizes now that he never has. The bus pulls up in front of the house. Laura says she'll keep Peter from getting custody of Timmy if it takes her dying breath.

3.

When he's alone, David opens the envelope. Inside is a note that says: "I saw you making love to Vanessa last night, saw everything you did to her. Saw you kill her." Stunned, David closes his door and dials Vanessa's number. An elderly man answers and identifies himself as Vanessa's father. He sounds upset. When David asks to speak to her, her father breaks down and says she's dead, murdered. The police are looking for the man she was with last night. He did this to her. David slams down the receiver as if it's suddenly red hot.

4.

"The ship has been overtaken by pirates!" Aunt Cora blurts out, and in the next instant the door bursts open and one of the pirates stands there, filthy, leering. He pushes Aunt Cora aside and grabs Victoria, nuzzling her breasts. She'll make a tasty prize for the captain, he says. She stomps on his foot and bites his hand, and as he cries out she flies past him, down the corridor and up the stairs. On deck, sailors and pirates struggle wildly, the boards running scarlet.

Failure

In section #1, the failure consists of the lead's inability to undo or deny the crisis. He must accept that his life has just turned upside down.

1.

Without returning to her classroom, Billi gets in her car and drives home in a daze. Two police officers are waiting for her, the same ones who were waiting for her at school. They tell Billi what happened at the convenience store. Then they hand her a shopping bag Stephen was carrying when the bullet hit him. In the bag is a pair of new slippers, clearly a Christmas present for Billi. She lowers her face to the slippers and weeps.

2.

Timmy appears and steps down from the bus. Laura runs toward him, but suddenly Peter rushes past her and lifts a laughing Timmy high into the air, then drops him into his silver convertible. Peter tells Timmy they're going for a little ride. "Bye, Mommy!" Peter says, smiling though his gaze is cold. Laura screams Timmy's name. The car takes off with a squeal of tires.

3.

David drives to Vanessa's house. The police have cordoned it off. He switches on the car radio and hears that the police are seeking David Williamson, the person last seen with Vanessa Houghton, who was found hanging by a leather strap from the ceiling of her bedroom.

4.

A thick arm grabs Victoria around the waist. It's the pirate she bit. He nibbles her ear, holding her while another man, clearly the pirate captain, approaches. He laughs, cupping one of her breasts, and says he'll keep her for himself. Then he orders the other pirate to take her to his new cabin below.

New Goal (or Go to a Reaction Section)

You don't actually show your section character devising this new goal in the action section, but you must decide what this goal will be. If your next section will be a reaction section, you needn't devise this goal now at all; you'll devise it in the reaction section. Otherwise, indicate the new goal here.

Since the failure in section #1 is one of the most devastating failures in your novel, a reaction section is definitely in order. Leave this area blank on section sheet #1.

Figure 3 is an example of section sheet #1 as it might look for Sara Bradford's story.

SECTION SHEET #2

Fold down the left-hand flap and enter your lead's name at the top of the sheet as the section character.

Failure From Character's Last Action Section

The first thing you must do in a reaction section is briefly restate exactly what terrible thing has just happened to the section character. The reason for this is the reader must be told exactly what an especially devastating failure means to the character.

For example, let's say an action section ends with a character discovering that the Earth-owned space station he has traveled light-years to reach has been ravaged by disease, leaving the entire crew dead. The action section would end with this gruesome discovery—certainly a failure devastating enough to warrant a reaction sheet.

What the reader doesn't know yet is that the dead crew means more to the character than just a dead crew. You've decided that if the disease has reached and invaded this space station, it has undoubtedly also reached all the other space stations in this part of the galaxy; it's just that kind of disease. The reader has no way of knowing exactly what this failure represents unless you tell him, and you do so at the beginning of the reaction section.

Whether or not the failure needs explaining, restate it briefly here, as in the following examples:

SARA BRADFORD'S SECTION SHEET #1

Action	FROM # #1 SECTION CHARACTER: Sara Bradford	Reaction
	Where: Her office at the station	
	When: Monday morning	
Goal From Character's Last Section		Failure From Character's Last Action Section
Against	Connie Farnsworth, Lance's administrative assistant	With
Conflict	Sara's dealing with some routine police matters when Connie, whom Sara barely knows, arrives at the station unexpectedly. Connie, clearly nervous, says she's been working up her courage to speak to Sara. After much hesitation she reveals she has good reason to believe Lance is involved in things he shouldn't be involved in. He may even be a member of the Ku Klux Klan. Sara laughs and says that's impossible, ludicrous. Connie says she wouldn't make such a statement without being reasonably sure. She says she cares about Lance and is only telling Sara so she can prevent Lance from destroying himself and his career. Amazed at this woman and her nonsense, Sara thanks her and sees her out.	Emotional Rational
Failure (Unless Opposition)	But when Connie is gone, Sara sits stunned. Connie's accusation is impossible to believe of the man she loves, lives with, thought she knew.	
New Goal (OR Go to a Reaction Section)		New Goal

TO #2

Figure 3

Stephen is dead.

Peter has kidnapped their son.

Vanessa has been murdered, and the cops think David did it.

Victoria is a prisoner of the pirates' captain.

The disease known as Zartak-4 has decimated all the space stations in Sector 8 of the Piroan Galaxy.

With

Who is with this character as he reacts to the failure? It isn't mandatory for another character to be present. What would be natural and believable under the circumstances?

Billi, in her living room after the police have gone, would most likely remain alone.

Laura, on the other hand, might call her best friend or her mother or her sister—and the one she calls would most likely be the confidant—as she wildly reacts to what Peter has just done.

Poor David can't confide in anyone—or can he? Who's his confidant? Can David reach him or her to talk privately about what's happened to Vanessa? Would he be likely to seek out this person, given the nature of their relationship? It would all depend on how you'd defined the confidant earlier.

Victoria will undoubtedly be alone as she reacts to her crisis. She'll be locked in the pirate's cabin.

If your lead will be with another character—not necessarily the confidant, but whoever would be likely—put that character's name here.

Emotional

Describe the character's emotional response to the failure.

1.

Billi is numb, still floating through her life as if Stephen will walk in at any moment. It's all too crazy, some kind of cruel joke.

2.

Laura calls her neighbor and best friend, Rachel, who hurries over. Laura is horrified. All the hate she has felt toward Peter since their encounter rushes to the surface.

3.

David is shocked and terrified. Shocked that someone else may have had the same kind of relationship with Vanessa that he did—except *that* someone killed her. Terrified because the police believe he did it, and he's not at all sure he'll be able to prove otherwise.

4.

Victoria is wild with fear—fear of what the pirates will do to poor old Aunt Cora, fear of what their captain will do to her.

5.

Jeremy, back on his own ship with Dr. Harvey, his second in command, is stunned at the immense loss of life, news of which never reached Earth.

Rational

Describe the character's analyzing and option-weighing process.

1.

Billi tries to pull herself together, tries to make herself understand that Stephen is really gone—just like that. These things happen. You see them on the news all the time; you just don't expect them to happen to you. She hopes he didn't feel anything. How exactly did it happen? she wonders. She's afraid to know. If only he didn't feel any pain, her wonderful, sweet Stephen who will never come home.

2.

Laura tells Rachel she should have expected something like this from Peter. She should have seen it coming. She just never imagined he'd pull something like this, the bastard. She hopes Timmy isn't scared. Laura has always protected him from Peter's violent side. He's probably got Timmy at his parents' apartment downtown. She could call the police, but the thought of all of South Ridge knowing her sordid business horrifies her. It would also horrify Peter, the big-shot lawyer. Maybe she should go to his apartment and threaten to tell the press everything if he doesn't give Timmy back. She'd never really do it, but Peter wouldn't know that.

3.

David thinks back to the times he's been with Vanessa. She never mentioned any other man she was seeing, but then, Vanessa could be secretive; she could have had a whole other life and he wouldn't have known about it. Come to think of it, she did have a whole other life—her job at Digicomm. He used to tease her about being the proper executive by day and the wild sex animal by night, especially when they got heavy into the Game. He remembers commenting that her colleagues would be shocked if they knew the other her, and she had answered with a smile and told him he'd be surprised. What the hell did she mean by that? Was she seeing someone else? Maybe he should just go to the police and tell them everything. After all, he *didn't* kill her, and playing the Game wasn't illegal—at least not in New York. But would the cops listen to him? For some reason they already thought he did it—or did they? Maybe all they wanted to do was ask him some questions because he was the last person to see her alive, not counting the killer. What the hell should he do? Talk to her father? He might know something. Who wrote that note? The same person who killed Vanessa and is framing him. . . .

4.

Victoria looks around the tiny cabin and ponders what to do. The door is locked and there is no porthole. She could find something to hurt the pirate with and attack him as he comes in. But would he simply overpower her? Perhaps she should pretend to play along and then catch him off guard. But even a little playing along meant he'd do hideous things to her. What about a bribe! Pirates love money. She's a rich woman. She could promise him a large payment in exchange for her release; she'd even sign a paper swearing to it. And what about ransom money? Uncle Montague would gladly pay for her return.

5.

Jeremy tells Dr. Harvey that Earth Control will be devastated at this news. And there's no question as to what they will tell him to do: Find the core organism that is present in every Zartak-4 colony and destroy it. As an officer, he would have to obey that order, even though it could mean his death. He could refuse; after all, the game has changed. Disease hunting isn't what he agreed to do. And yet, an officer obeys commands—unless he just walks away, quits, disappears. Of course, if he did that, he could never return to Earth again. He'd never see Jasmara again. He couldn't bear that. Besides, running away isn't his style.

New Goal

At the end of the reaction section you *do* show your section character devising a new section goal.

Note that in section #2, however, your lead sets *two* goals:

1. The story goal—the objective she will be striving to achieve *throughout the novel.*

2. A new section goal.

You already devised your lead's story goal when you created your story idea. The story goal begins with "S/he decides s/he must. . . ." Enter that goal here on the reaction section sheet.

1.

Billi decides she must get through this devastation and get on with her life because it's what Stephen would have wanted.

2.

Laura decides she must get Timmy back.

3.

David decides he must find out who killed Vanessa to clear himself.

4.

Victoria decides she must escape from the pirates and get herself and Aunt Cora to safety.

5.

Jeremy decides he must find and destroy Zartak-4's core organism before it wipes out the entire Piroan Galaxy.

Phrase the new section goal like this:

S/he will _____

in order to

_____ .

1.

Billi will bravely face the police, answer their questions, learn what happened to Stephen, in order to start dealing with this tragedy.

2.

Laura will go to Peter's parents' apartment and threaten him with a scandal in order to force him to give Timmy back to her.

3.

David will speak to Vanessa's father in order to try to find out what really happened after David left Vanessa's apartment last night.

4.

Victoria will pretend to be willing in order to buy some time during which she and Aunt Cora can escape.

5.

Jeremy will go back into the space station and look for clues in order to trace the disease's present location.

Figure 4 is Sara Bradford's section sheet #2.

SARA BRADFORD'S SECTION SHEET #2

FROM #1

Action	#2	Reaction
	SECTION CHARACTER: Sara Bradford	
	Where: A café on the way home from work	
	When: Early Monday evening	
Goal From Character's Last Section	Connie has accused Lance of being a Klan member.	Failure From Character's Last Action Section
Against	Rosie Pike	With
Conflict	Sara tells Rosie she's furious—how dare Connie make such an accusation! The dried-up old witch probably has the hots for Lance and is hurt because he barely notices her. But to suggest that about Lance—a respected senator, a man famous for his liberalism and sense of fairness. It's pure slander.	Emotional
	She can't just ignore it. She could talk to Lance, but for some reason she doesn't want to. Why? Rosie asks. Because he'll just deny it? Angry, Sara says it would hurt him terribly if he thought she believed he could ever do such a thing. Yet, Rosie says, Sara's not just forgetting the whole thing. Ignoring this, Sara says she should probably just keep an eye on Lance, find out what he's doing that would give Connie such ideas.	Rational
Failure (Unless Opposition)		
New Goal (OR Go to a Reaction Section)	(1) Sara decides she must find out if Lance is a member of the KKK, if he's living a secret life. (2) Sara will watch Lance and follow him the next time he goes out on one of his unexplained appointments in order to find out if he's really attending Klan meetings.	New Goal

TO #3

Figure 4

SECTION SHEET #3

Section #3 is an action section, again featuring your lead.

Goal From Character's Last Action Section

Insert your character's section goal at the end of section #2.

1.

To bravely face the police, answer their questions, learn what happened to Stephen, in order to start dealing with this tragedy.

2.

To go to Peter's apartment and threaten him with a scandal in order to force him to give Timmy back to her.

3.

To speak with Vanessa's father in order to try to find out what really happened after David left Vanessa's apartment last night.

4.

To pretend to be willing in order to buy some time during which she and Aunt Cora can escape.

5.

To go back into the space station and look for clues in order to trace the disease's present location.

Against

Your section character (in this case your lead), in trying to achieve the short-term goal, must confront another character you've already created (it can be, but doesn't have to be, the opposition). List here this other character; for example:

1.
The police

2.
Peter

3.
Vanessa's father

4.

The pirate captain

5.

Dr. Harvey (who refuses to risk his life by accompanying Jeremy)

Conflict

The conflict phase constitutes the bulk of the action section. The conflict is the essence of the section, just as it is the essence of the novel as a whole. Readers want to witness a good struggle; they want to really wonder whether the section character will achieve her short-term goal. The opposing character must have a good reason for wanting the section character to fail in her mission to achieve her short-term goal, and the opposing character's behavior will be driven by that desire.

Outline the main points of the struggle—anything from an argument to a physical fight to a chase—between these two characters.

1.

Billi finds the police strangely unforthcoming with information about exactly how Stephen died. They are asking her questions, but they're not at all the questions Billi expected. The police want to know if Stephen had ever talked about needing money badly, if he had any sort of drug problem, if he had any history of break-ins or robberies! Billi insists on knowing why they're asking her these things. She realizes now there's something they're not telling her. But she won't ask anything, mustn't give them any ideas. She demands to know what happened in that convenience store; as his mother she has a right to know. They ask her to answer their questions first, and then they'll answer hers. No, she tells them, no to everything. He was a good boy who went to junior college and had a beer or two with his buddies on Friday nights.

2.

When Laura gets to Peter's parents' apartment, no one answers the door. She wonders if anyone's home, but then she calls Peter's and Timmy's names and Timmy runs to the door, crying for her. But Peter won't open the door. He tells her to go home, that she's wasting her time. He's keeping Timmy, just as he said he would, and she can do anything she wants, go to any court, but she'll never get him back. Laura, frantic, hating to talk through a door, begs him to open it but he won't. So she warns him through the door that if he doesn't hand Timmy over right now, the next stops she makes will be the newspaper—where she'll spill the whole story of the town's prominent lawyer taking the law into his own hands and kidnapping his own son— and then the police station, where they'll agree he's broken the law and come back here with her. Still he won't open the door.

3.

David has convinced Vanessa's father to meet him secretly. David asks him what happened last night. A hostile Mr. Houghton says that's exactly what he wants David to tell him. David explains that he and Vanessa went to dinner at Lily's Rolls Royce, then went back to Vanessa's apartment. "To play your filthy sex games?" the old man asks. David ignores this, says simply that he left Vanessa's apartment at 1:15 A.M., and that when he left, she was very much alive. Houghton says he doesn't believe a word David says, and he refuses to tell David anything of what he knows of last night—and clearly he knows something.

4.

The cabin door bursts open and the pirate captain enters. Victoria puts on a brave face. He grabs her, savagely mauls her, pinches her breasts, kisses her so hard that tears come to her eyes. But then, to Victoria's surprise, he suddenly stops, busying himself at the desk in the corner of the cabin. She must distract him, make him think she's willing. Daringly she tells him she's always wondered what it would be like to make love to a pirate, a *real* man. He turns and tells her that her tricks won't work on him. He's not the drooling clod she thinks he is. He's an educated man—Oxford—and even studied the law. And it's not for her luscious body that he wants Victoria. In fact, it's not even for her money, though he knows she has a lot of that; he's after a much bigger prize. Victoria demands to know why, then, he has massacred the ship's crew and detained her and her aunt.

5.

Jeremy has finally persuaded the reluctant Dr. Harvey to accompany him back onto the space station. This time, fully suited against the disease, they begin a thorough inspection. Dr. Harvey makes it as far as the second ring of habitation units, then suddenly blurts out that he can't go on; it's too dangerous. Jeremy knows what he means. The disease's usual pattern is to ravage its victims and move on, but it's entirely possible that part of the disease has remained here, perhaps awaiting more victims. But Jeremy needs a second person to help him conduct the inspection, and he has given Dr. Harvey strict orders. He tells the other man to get ahold of himself, and they enter the habitation units, finding victim after victim of Zartak-4, each with his skin rotted away to expose the tissue and bones beneath—the disease's trademark. At the sight of a particularly gruesome corpse, Dr. Harvey bolts from the room. Jeremy catches him. Dr. Harvey screams that these are the worst cases of the disease he's ever seen; Jeremy knows as well as he does that the disease is probably still here. Jeremy says that's why they're suited against it. He convinces Dr. Harvey to continue, promising that as soon as they've got some indication of the disease's present location they'll leave.

Failure

Whatever form the failure takes, it must come swiftly and suddenly for full dramatic impact.

1.

Then the police tell Billi they had been watching Stephen for some time. He was running an extensive ring of brutal holdup men in the city, and today he decided to pull off one of the robberies himself. Unfortunately, the store clerk had a gun handy and managed to shoot Stephen in the head at the exact same time that Stephen shot the clerk in the chest. It's all on video. Fortunately for the clerk and the police, the clerk's still alive, and he's going to make it.

2.

Peter tells Laura it doesn't matter what she tells the newspaper because he's leaving South Ridge forever—with Timmy. He can't risk exposing the boy to Laura any further. And as for the police, he's already told them about Laura's drug problem and the string of men she's been bringing to the house—and about how she's been harassing him. Suddenly the door opens, and at the same time, at the street, a police car pulls up. Peter thanks the officers for coming, throws up his hands, and indicating poor, crying Timmy, asks if they could please take Laura away so he and his son and his parents can have a little peace. The officers, clearly friends of Peter's, assure him that they'll take care of it. Peter smiles and shuts the door.

3.

As David, frustrated, gets up to leave, the old man says Vanessa told him all about David—that he had a vicious temper and was wildly jealous. Vanessa told her father that when she tried to break off their relationship, David told her that she'd be dead first, that she'd be his or no one's. And, Houghton says, he's told all this to the cops.

4.

Because, the captain says, he knows that Victoria is an expert on the Pearl Islands and their history. If so, she undoubtedly knows of the fantastic treasure buried there a thousand years ago by the islands' early inhabitants. That's all just a legend, Victoria says; it's not real. Ah, but there she's wrong, he says. He knows the treasure is real and he knows where it is. What he needs is someone who knows the natives, who are guarding it, well enough to lead them into his trap.

5.

Jeremy has no sooner said these words than the ceiling panel above Dr. Harvey's head bursts open and a gray phosphorescent tentacle—Jeremy knows it's Zartak-4—drops straight down and pierces Dr. Harvey's helmet with its needlelike tip. Dr. Harvey's eyes roll back in his head, and in the next instant his skin is rotting from his skull. Jeremy turns and runs for his ship.

Figure 5 is Sara Bradford's section sheet #3.

To Recap
- To prevent stalling while writing your novel, you must first plot it in its entirety.
- The classic Aristotelian novel structure is (1) the beginning (the first quarter of the book), (2) the middle (comprising half the book's length), and (3) the end (the last quarter of the book).
- Determine your novel's ideal length and create the appropriate number of section sheets.
- A section is a unit of story action in your novel.
- In an action section, a character seeks to achieve a short-term goal.
- In a reaction section, a character reacts to what happened in the previous action section.
- In section #1, your lead experiences the crisis.
- In section #2, your lead reacts to the crisis by setting a story goal and a section goal.
- In section #3, your lead springs into action, pursuing the section goal just set.

SARA BRADFORD'S SECTION SHEET #3

FROM #2

Action	#3	Reaction
	SECTION CHARACTER: Sara Bradford	
	Where: Sara and Lance's home	
	When: 8 P.M. Tuesday	
Goal From Character's Last Section	To watch Lance and follow him the next time he goes out on one of his unexplained appointments, in order to find out if he's really attending Klan meetings.	Failure From Character's Last Action Section
Against	Lance	With
Conflict	When Lance tells Sara he has to go out, she says she's had Juanita make a special dinner and couldn't he stay home? He says he's sorry but it's not something he can cancel. Sara asks him what's so important but he laughs and says it'll do her good not to know everything. Sara gives up but watches him leave, and as soon as he drives off she jumps into her Jeep and follows him at a safe distance. A mile from the house she loses him. A minute later he pulls up behind her, gets out, and gets into Sara's Jeep. He says he resents her following him; if she doesn't trust him, he wants out of their marriage.	Emotional
		Rational
Failure (Unless Opposition)	Sara tries to apologize but he says he's extremely upset and will spend the next few nights at his club while he sorts out his feelings about this situation.	
New Goal (OR Go to a Reaction Section)	Sara will drop the whole issue, in order to prove to Lance that she does trust him.	New Goal

TO #5

Figure 5

Interweaving Story Lines

In This Step
- The lead's subplot
- Other characters' story lines
- Rotating story lines

Up to now you've been concerned only with your lead and his main story line. At this point you'll begin new story threads— a subplot for your lead and a story line for each of your other viewpoint characters, through whose awareness and perceptions you will plan and write sections. In this step you'll learn how to get these story lines started and keep them going, interweaving them for maximum dramatic impact.

Why do you need a subplot and other story lines? A subplot for your lead adds depth and texture to a novel. It gives your reader other issues to worry about when she's not worrying about how the main story line will resolve itself. A subplot involving your novel's lead also makes a novel more realistic. In real life we don't pursue a goal in a vacuum, unaffected by other events and situations in our lives.

ADVANTAGES OF SUBPLOTS

The most effective subplots intertwine with and are somehow related to the main story line. Think of a subplot as a formalized way of showing that life is complicated, that how we strive to achieve our goals is to some extent a function of what else is happening to us.

In John Lutz's thriller *SWF Seeks Same* (the basis for the movie *Single White Female*), Allie Jones, the lead, is a hungry software entrepreneur living in New York City. Early in the story, Allie meets Mike Mayfair, a prospective customer who's more interested in Allie than in her software system. As Lutz develops the main story line—Allie, having kicked out her live-in boyfriend, needs a roommate and takes in the psychopathic Hedra Carlson—he also keeps the Mike Mayfair subplot going. When Allie visits Mayfair's office to tutor him in using the system, he makes his move, and Allie rejects him, thereby losing the account. Much later, when a penniless Allie is fleeing the murderous Hedra, Lutz makes clever use of the Mayfair subplot by having Allie break into Mayfair's apartment and steal several items that she later sells. (One of the items is Mayfair's laptop computer—a nice touch of irony.) Not only has Mayfair's presence in Allie's life affected how she behaves in dire straits, but Lutz has also achieved a satisfying justice as Allie uses Mayfair instead of Mayfair using Allie. This is an excellent example of a subplot that relates to *and* influences the main story line.

Story lines involving characters other than your lead also add depth and texture to a novel if only because they show us the private actions of people involved in the lead's life and in his pursuit of the story goal. Once again we get a more realistic picture of how life works: We strive for goals in the context of how others in our lives behave, not in a vacuum.

But these other-character story lines can do much more. We've all read novels in which a character reflects on the lead— something she's said or done, her situation, even how she looks. This gives us insights into the lead that we could never get from within the lead's own consciousness and adds depth to the story: We see ways in which the lead may not perceive her world or situation objectively or realistically. And, of course, we learn how the other character perceives the lead's situation and what he intends to do about it.

This leads to another important function other-character story lines can perform. By showing the reader things the lead doesn't know about, you give the reader a superior position and create what's called dramatic irony—when the lead doesn't know something the audience knows. The most obvious use of this device is to create suspense by showing that a character intends to harm or oppose the lead. The lead doesn't know, and the reader bites her nails waiting for the confrontation or hoping the lead catches on in time. It's a device as old as storytelling— and it always works.

Jackie Collins used this device quite effectively in her block-buster *Hollywood Wives*. Interwoven among the stories of women seeking power and passion in Hollywood's make-believe world is a dark, gritty story line about Deke Andrews, a delusional murderer making his way west across the country from Philadelphia, frantic to reach California. Collins has lent additional subtlety to this device in two ways: (1) We don't know why Deke wants to get to California, so (2) we don't know which character in Hollywood Deke has a connection to. At the end, when these questions are answered, it's a real shocker.

Other-character story lines also serve to flesh out these characters themselves. They are shown pursuing story goals of their own; how they go about these pursuits characterizes them for the reader. When the reader knows these characters well, she better understands what motivates them when they oppose the lead. And when the reader understands the motivations of both the lead and an opposing character, the confrontation between them becomes more believable.

You'll have a lot of freedom when you develop your lead's subplot and other viewpoint characters' story lines. With only a few exceptions, you can devise any goal for each of these story lines as long as that goal relates in some way to the lead's main story line. (The opposition, the confidant and the romantic involvement have prescribed goals.) You can even delay showing the reader how a story line relates to the lead's main story line (as Jackie Collins did with Deke) as long as you do eventually make the connection.

The subplots and story lines that don't work never really connect to the lead's main story line. The reader patiently follows these threads, trusting they'll converge at some point—but they never do. A novel like this is really just a braid of several stories within a single cover. Don't make this mistake; remember that readers assume from the very existence of a subordinate story line that it will fit somehow into the lead's journey to her story goal.

SECTION SHEET #4: CREATING YOUR LEAD'S SUBPLOT

Section #4 is where you'll begin your lead's subplot. This is another action section—an exception to the rule that says an especially devastating failure calls for a reaction section. The reason for this exception is that this section is not about your lead's main story line; it's the beginning of the lead's subplot, and any new story line begins with an action section.

The lead's subplot is a separate, self-contained story thread related to the lead's main story line. How do you determine your lead's subplot?

• If you decided earlier to have a romantic involvement in your novel, that is your lead's subplot.

• If your novel has no romantic involvement, you must devise a subplot. Make sure it relates to the lead's main story line.

The Lead's Subplot: Romantic Involvement

The romantic involvement's story goal is to win or keep the lead's love. This means that in every section containing your lead and the romantic involvement, the romantic involvement's goal will be aimed toward this larger goal. The lead's goal will be to resist the romantic involvement's efforts.

A romantic subplot has a special set of rules. Right from the start, your lead and the romantic involvement must feel a sense of attraction that will grow and produce romantic and/or sexual tension as the subplot progresses. This attraction and tension may prompt them to act on their feelings in whatever way or ways are in character and are appropriate to the situation.

However, right from the start two other elements must be present to generate the conflict between these two characters and thus prevent their committing to each other. These elements are the *internal conflict* and the *external conflict*.

The Internal Conflict. This conflict refers to an emotional resistance within each character which makes him or her hesitant or unwilling to enter into, continue with or commit to a romantic or sexual relationship.

For example, a woman whose firefighter husband died in a fire might be terrified of committing to a man she might lose due to his similarly dangerous profession. A man whose wife betrayed his trust by having extramarital affairs and then finally left him might be unwilling to open his heart again.

An internal conflict can take any number of forms, as long as it constitutes a *conflict* to the character's attraction to the other character. Of course, the internal conflicts for your lead and romantic involvement will depend on the backgrounds you've created for them.

Sara Bradford's romantic involvement is Eric Montero. Eric's daughter, Wanda, lives with him, as does Eric's mother, Queenie, who takes care of Wanda. Ursula, Eric's ex-wife, is out of the picture. Also, until the possibility of a relationship with Sara arose, Eric frequented bars every night, picking up different women.

It's safe to surmise that Eric's relationship with Ursula was less than happy. We can go back and add details that would give Eric his internal conflict. For example, we could decide that Ursula grew bored with Eric's stodgy work life and craved an excitement he couldn't give her. So she fooled around with other men, ultimately right under Eric's nose, at which point he threw her out. What hurt Eric most was not Ursula's infidelity (though that did hurt) but how her lack of concern for Wanda traumatized the child. The girl still cries when she remembers the things her mother did—like the time Ursula left Wanda alone in the apartment to keep a rendezvous with a boyfriend, and the cat knocked over a candle in the kitchen and a fire started. A neighbor rescued poor Wanda (and the cat) from the smoke-filled apartment.

So, as you can imagine, Eric refuses to commit to a new woman because he will not permit Wanda to be hurt again. In fact, he doesn't even let Wanda meet any of the women he sees.

Review the character fact list for your romantic involvement and see if you can find an internal conflict there—or the seeds of one. If you have to, add material, as we did for Eric, to create the basis of an internal conflict.

Now follow the same procedure for your lead. For Sara, the internal conflict is easy. She's married, which for a lead is a big deal; remember, she's virtuous. Of course, eventually Sara will realize that Lance is a creep and Eric is the man for her—as your lead and romantic involvement will do—but at the beginning it's simply that she's married to Lance, for better or worse, that holds her back. (By the way, you'd think Eric would understand where she's coming from, given his experience with Ursula; but he won't understand—he wants Sara that badly—and his lack of understanding can make for some juicy conflict between them.)

The External Conflict. As if the internal conflict weren't enough, there must be an external conflict also keeping the lead and the romantic involvement from getting together. This external conflict is an outside, *situational* element that stands as an obstacle to a relationship.

For example, a woman has come west to bring to justice the gunfighter she believes shot her father, then, to her own amazement, finds herself attracted to the gunfighter—that's external conflict. A police detective who finds himself falling in love with a suspect; a teacher attracted to a student—these are both external conflicts.

For Sara and Eric, the external conflict is that she is his boss; romantic relations between them are strictly forbidden.

Review the character fact lists for your lead and romantic involvement and, if necessary, add material that would create an external conflict between them.

The Lead's Subplot: No Romantic Involvement

If your novel has no romantic involvement, you need a secondary goal for your lead. Once again, your lead seeks

- Possession of something (e.g., a person, an object, information), or

• Relief from something (e.g., fear, pain, sadness, loneliness, domination, oppression).

Review your lead's character fact list, looking for subplot ideas. Chances are you'll find you've already planted some useful seeds.

Sara Bradford volunteers at Helping Hand, a children's shelter. If she had no romantic involvement, a possible subplot might center on this work. For instance, Sara might encounter an especially endearing child who has suffered at the hands of his abusive father, who is intent on getting his son back. Sara's subplot goal could be to place the boy in a loving foster home, out of his father's grasp.

Here are some other examples of leads' subplots. They take the same form as the main story idea, though they needn't incorporate an opposition.

1.

Billi realizes that a sinister-looking young man has been watching her house. She decides she must find out who he is and what his involvement with Stephen was.

2.

Laura's boss, who dislikes her and has been looking for a reason to fire her, is using Laura's erratic behavior to build a case against her. Laura decides she must keep up the illusion of normalcy at work; she can't afford to lose her job.

3.

David is so distraught at Vanessa's murder and the events surrounding it that he seeks confidential counseling to sort out what really happened—he's not so sure anymore. He decides he must find out the truth about his feelings toward Vanessa.

4.

Aunt Cora is suffering terrible nervous strain as a prisoner of the pirates. Victoria decides she must keep the old dear distracted to ease her anxiety.

5.

Jeremy finds one creature still alive on one of the disease-ravaged space stations: a zhalster, a small furry animal that is native to the planet Yy. Jeremy decides he must watch the animal and try to figure out why it was immune to Zartak-4.

Carrying Over Emotion

At the end of section #3, your lead experienced a failure. Ordinarily, on this next action sheet, you would show your lead acting on a new short-term goal resulting from that failure.

But here, as you begin your lead's subplot, you're not going to do that. Bring from the last section only how the lead would feel—his emotional state as a result of the failure. Then, with your character in this emotional state, begin your subplot.

Leave "Goal From Character's Last Section" blank.

For "Against," enter the name of the character against whom the lead's subplot puts him in conflict. If you have a romantic subplot, that character is your romantic involvement.

For Billi, it's the sinister-looking young man.
For Laura, it's her scheming boss.
For David, it's the psychiatrist.
For Victoria, it's Aunt Cora.
For Jeremy, it's the zhalster.

In "Conflict," show your lead in his emotional state from his failure in section #3, trying to attain his subplot goal.

For example, you'd show Billi, stunned and incredulous at what the police said, catching the young man watching the house and, reckless in her distraught state, running outside to speak to him.

You'd show Laura, badly shaken after Peter's manipulation of the police, in a meeting with her boss. She's trying to appear calm and businesslike, trying to keep her hands from shaking, as he watches her closely and finally asks if she's been getting enough sleep—or if perhaps her job is becoming too much for her.

You'd show David, sweating profusely, terrified he'll be caught, sitting facing the psychiatrist, who's not sympathetic. In fact, David wonders if he can trust the man at all. Has he made a terrible mistake coming here?

You'd show Victoria, disgusted at the captain's high-handed tactics, trying not to let these feelings show as she plays a game of Old Maid with Aunt Cora, who keeps insisting the pirates will murder them both.

You'd show Jeremy, professionally calm as ever—even after what happened to Dr. Harvey—studying the zhalster, baffled as to why this small creature with no central circulatory organ has escaped the ravages of Zartak-4.

Failure

Show the failure as usual.

1.

The young man takes off, Billi's cries echoing in the empty darkness.

2.

Despite Laura's assurances that she's just fine, her boss says he's been unhappy with the quality of her work lately, and after what he's seen today, he's going to have to speak to his boss about her.

3.

David's psychiatrist says David is obviously upset, but he wonders if David has a clear grasp of his problem. The doctor believes David simply needs a tranquilizer so he can calm down and rationally separate fact from fancy. He writes David a prescription for Xanax and says their session is over.

4.

Just as Victoria is assuring Aunt Cora that the pirates have no intention of hurting either of them, a pirate bursts in and says the captain has ordered him to "entertain" Aunt Cora until Victoria changes her mind about helping the captain find the Pearl Islands treasure.

5.

Jeremy, stumped and exhausted, puts the zhalster back in its cage.

For an example of how a romantic subplot would begin, see Sara Bradford's section sheet #4 in Figure 6.

SECTION SHEET #5

In section #5, you return to the lead's main story line, which you left hanging at the end of section #3.

As you weave story lines, you'll want an easy way to track where they pick up and leave off. That's what the "FROM #" and "TO #" at the top and bottom of the section sheet are for.

At the bottom of section sheet #3, enter a 5 so it reads "To #5." At the top of section sheet #5, enter a 3 so it reads "FROM #3." This signifies that the story line leaves off in section #3 and picks up in section #5.

From now on, when you leave story lines and pick them up later, use these guides to indicate how the story lines run.

Section #5, an action section, picks up from the failure at the end of section #3. Your lead has a new section goal and moves through the conflict phase as usual. Once again, the events of section #4 will undoubtedly affect her mental state as she moves through this phase.

To illustrate:

1.

Agitated at losing the sinister young man, Billi reacts to what the police said by searching Stephen's room for signs of a secret life.

2.

Laura—convinced she's going to lose her job, chain-smoking as she curses her boss up and down—reacts to Peter's high-handed manipulation by seeking out a lawyer who can tell her her rights.

3.

David, calmer on the Xanax but baffled by the psychiatrist's advice, reacts to what Mr. Houghton said by seeking out a

SARA BRADFORD'S SECTION SHEET #4

FROM #

Action	#4	Reaction
	SECTION CHARACTER: Sara Bradford	
	Where: The station	
	When: Wednesday morning	
Goal From Character's Last Section		Failure From Character's Last Action Section
Against	Eric Montero	With
Conflict	Sara, badly shaken after her encounter last night with Lance, is jumpy and short tempered at work. She barks an order at Eric, who reacts by getting right in her face and asking just who she thinks she's talking to. She apologizes, explaining she's got some problems at home. For the first time, as they stand this close to each other, electricity flows between them. Their faces remain together a moment too long, each knowing what the other is thinking. Sara repeats that she's sorry and that they'd both better get back to work.	Emotional Rational
Failure (Unless Opposition)	Eric, giving Sara a meaningful look, says he's sure she *is* sorry, and saunters out of her office.	
New Goal (OR Go to a Reaction Section)	Sara will adopt a cool, professional manner in dealing with Eric from now on in order to prevent an encounter like this one from occurring again.	New Goal

TO #7

Figure 6

close friend of Vanessa's in an attempt to find out what was really going on in her life.

4.

Victoria is worried to death about poor, dear old Aunt Cora, who has been dragged away by the pirates and whose heart surely cannot take much more. Victoria tries to bargain with the captain, offering to draw him all the maps he needs if he'll let her and Aunt Cora go.

5.

Jeremy, still confounded as to what kept the zhalster alive, takes measures to plant timed explosives on the space station and detach his ship from the station in preparation for blowing it—and the Zartak-4—up.

Section sheet #5 ends with the failure as usual.
Figure 7 shows Sara Bradford's section sheet #5.

OTHER CHARACTERS' SUBPLOTS

Thus far in your plotting you've created sections that focus on your lead, whether her main story line or her subplot. We've been seeing the story exclusively from the lead's viewpoint; the action has centered on the lead's goals.

In section #6 you'll introduce your first (or only, depending on the length of your novel) subplot centering on another character. Like the lead, this character will have his own action and reaction sections in which he will set short-term goals in pursuit of his story goal.

When planning other characters' subplots, you must first determine how many viewpoint characters (including the lead) your novel should have. The NovelMaster in Figure 1 (page 59) gives you this number. In the table, find your word-length range and read across to the column headed "VP Characters," where you'll find the correct number of viewpoint characters for your novel.

The next decision is harder: Who should your other viewpoint characters be? Sometimes a novel's genre provides the answer. For example, if you're writing a short contemporary romance, whose length would dictate two viewpoint characters, those two

SARA BRADFORD'S SECTION SHEET #5

FROM #3

Action	#5	Reaction
	SECTION CHARACTER: Sara Bradford	
	Where: Sara and Lance's home	
	When: Saturday morning	
Goal From Character's Last Section	To drop the whole issue, in order to prove to Lance that she does trust him.	Failure From Character's Last Action Section
Against	Lance	With
Conflict	Lance returns from his club just before lunch. The meal is pleasant but strained, each spouse careful not to say the wrong thing. Desperate to remove the tension, Sara suggests that they drive into New Orleans after lunch, to walk around, maybe visit some art galleries. Lance smiles suggestively and says he has a better idea. She's surprised but relieved that his feelings haven't changed. They go up to their bedroom and Lance undresses her, then himself. She begins to respond, but suddenly when she shuts her eyes it's Eric's face she sees. She forces herself to look at Lance as he makes love to her. But again, images of Eric intrude, images of *him* making love to her. Lance jokes that it's been too long since they've been together. Sara tries to lose herself in passion . . .	Emotional

Rational |
| Failure (Unless Opposition) | . . . when suddenly Lance stops. He's furious. Clearly things are still not right between them. He dresses quickly and walks out, slamming the door. | |
| New Goal (OR Go to a Reaction Section) | | New Goal |

TO #9

Figure 7

characters are always the lead and the romantic involvement. You would know this from your reading and perhaps from the publishers' guidelines.

If you're writing a historical romance of 120,000 words, you're allowed five viewpoint characters and would make the first two of them your lead and romantic involvement. In fact, any kind of romance would have the lead and romantic involvement as viewpoint characters.

Sometimes a novel's genre tells you which characters *not* to use as viewpoint characters. In any novel in which the actions of a character (usually the opposition) are kept secret, you must not use that character as a viewpoint character. In a murder mystery, for example, you would never use the murderer as a viewpoint character because then, privy to all his thoughts and feelings, the reader would know he was the murderer—a secret you can't reveal till the end!

In Agatha Christie's *The Murder of Roger Ackroyd*, the story's narrator turns out to be the murderer. Many readers have objected to this device as "cheating": We are led to believe that because this narrator is a viewpoint character, we know everything important about him. Yet the most important thing about him is saved to the end, purely for the author's convenience. It's a trick you shouldn't try.

So who are your viewpoint characters? Fill your allotted slots in this order:

- Your lead is always the first viewpoint character.

Romantic Involvement

- If you have a romantic involvement, he or she is *always* viewpoint character #2.

Opposition

- *If you have no romantic involvement*, your opposition is viewpoint character #2.
- *If you have a romantic involvement*, your opposition is viewpoint character #3.

- *If your novel requires an "invisible" opposition* (as explained above), skip the opposition as a viewpoint character entirely.

Confidant
- *If you have no romantic involvement and a "visible" opposition,* your confidant is viewpoint character #3.
- *If you have no romantic involvement and an "invisible" opposition,* your confidant is viewpoint character #2.
- *If you have a romantic involvement and an "invisible" opposition,* your confidant is viewpoint character #3.
- *If you have a romantic involvement and a "visible" opposition,* your confidant is viewpoint character #4.

If you're writing a novel requiring more viewpoint characters, select them from your list of additional characters. Choose the ones you believe will play the most important roles in your story, then create a character fact list for each.

When you've decided on all of your viewpoint characters, pull their character fact lists, write "VP" and the number (for example, "VP #3") at the top of each, put them in order and staple them together. Leave them within easy reach on your desk.

SECTION SHEET #6

Section #6 is an action section. The section character is your viewpoint character #2. You're looking at the story from *this* character's perspective now.

If you have a romantic involvement, he is viewpoint character #2 and was introduced in section #4. As a result of what happened in that section, he has set a new short-term goal that he will pursue now. He's thinking about or in some way reacting to what happened in section #4. Take him through the phases of the action section, ending with a failure for him.

If you have no romantic involvement, your viewpoint character #2 is the opposition—unless you have an "invisible" opposition—in which case your viewpoint character #2 is the confidant. You may or may not have introduced this character yet. If you have, remember that he'll be thinking about or in some way reacting to what happened in that section as he pursues his short-term goal in this section.

Since this may be your first section in which the opposition is the section character, note that in any sections containing the opposition, the opposition ends on a success, not a failure. On the section sheet, "(Unless Opposition)" appears under "Failure" to remind you of this.

Here are some examples of oppositions achieving their section goals.

1.

Let's say the sinister young man is Billi's opposition. Here he's thinking about being spotted and chased by Stephen's mother while he was watching her house to see what happened with the police, but more to get an idea of her schedule so he'd know when to search the place. Finally he does get in to search and takes an incriminating piece of evidence Stephen had hidden in his room—evidence that would have shown that Stephen was only a pawn in the sinister young man's game. Evidence that would have helped Billi. Opposition's section goal achieved.

2.

Peter is thinking about the encounter with Laura as he now makes plans to take Timmy away. Perhaps in this section he wants to convince the woman he's been seeing to let him use her house on Martha's Vineyard for a few weeks while he sorts things out. She resists, but at the end of the section she says yes—section goal achieved for the opposition.

3.

Let's say David's opposition is a man Vanessa worked with and who also got pulled into her kinky world, but things got out of hand. He's thinking about having sent David that note accusing him of killing Vanessa. He's remembering the argument he and Vanessa had before things got wild, before she was hanging there and gave him the mercy signal but he was hating her so much that he literally saw red.

He wanted her to die, and he couldn't believe it but she *was* dying, right there in front of him, and he was glad. Now, driven by all these thoughts and the fear of getting caught, he has set a section goal of further implicating David by planting an intimate garment of Vanessa's in David's office where David won't find it but the cops will. It's difficult at first to get in the office—the police have sealed it—but ultimately he manages to sneak in and plant the evidence. Opposition's section goal achieved.

4.

The pirate captain, frustrated at Victoria's stubbornness, sets a section goal of convincing her to help him by using the old lady. Victoria resists him at first, unwilling to succumb to his blackmail and calling his bluff. Then the captain gives a command, and from a distant place come Aunt Cora's screams. Victoria quickly agrees to help him. Opposition's section goal achieved.

5.

From another space station that has also been ravaged by Zartak-4, Volkag, who controls the movements of the disease, watches Jeremy by means of secret cameras mounted in every chamber of Jeremy's ship. Jeremy's discovery of the zhalster was unexpected, though Volkag is certain that Jeremy will never deduce the secret of the creature's survival. What's more important is that Jeremy must be stopped in his investigation. Volkag has planted an explosive device aboard Jeremy's ship, which Volkag intends to use now to destroy Jeremy. Volkag tries to detonate the device, encounters difficulty at first (conflict), and ultimately succeeds, seriously damaging Jeremy's ship. Opposition's section goal achieved.

Figure 8 is section sheet #6 from Sara Bradford's story. Since there's a romantic involvement, he's the section character.

SECTION SHEET #7

Section #7 is an action section dealing with the lead's subplot, which we left in section #4. Picking up from the failure in section

SARA BRADFORD'S SECTION SHEET #6

Action	FROM # #6 SECTION CHARACTER: Eric Montero	Reaction
	Where: At Helping Hand, the children's shelter	
	When: Monday afternoon	
Goal From Character's Last Section	To get close to Sara again, in order to relight the spark that ignited between them.	Failure From Character's Last Action Section
Against	Sara	With
Conflict	Sara has asked Eric to help her set up some tables and chairs that Sara convinced a local furniture dealer to donate to the shelter. Eric enjoys himself, joking with the children—who clearly love him—and chatting easily with Sara and Vicki Yost, who runs the shelter. When he and Sara are finished, they head for his car, in which they came, but Sara suggests they have a cup of coffee. Delighted at this sign that Sara shares his feelings, he agrees and they go to a nearby diner. Over coffee Eric makes his move. He says he wants to talk about what happened Wednesday morning. To his delight, she says she does, too. That kind of thing must never happen again, she says, or . . . or measures would have to be taken. Measures! Eric says. She knows damn well she's as interested as he is. Why doesn't she just let things go to where they want to go? He covers her hand with his. She pulls hers away and abruptly stands up, obviously upset.	Emotional Rational
Failure (Unless Opposition)	Try that again, she says, and he'll find himself out of a job. She tells him she'll find another way back to the station and walks out of the diner.	
New Goal (OR Go to a Reaction Section)	Eric will find the right quiet moment—away from work—in order to get close to Sara and let her see how right things could be between them if she'd only give him half a chance.	New Goal

TO #16

Figure 8

PATTERN OF STORY LINES

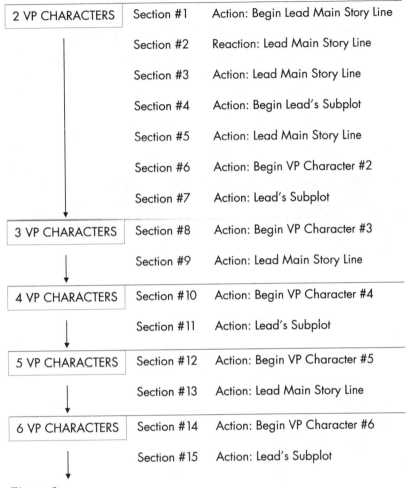

2 VP CHARACTERS	Section #1	Action: Begin Lead Main Story Line
	Section #2	Reaction: Lead Main Story Line
	Section #3	Action: Lead Main Story Line
	Section #4	Action: Begin Lead's Subplot
	Section #5	Action: Lead Main Story Line
	Section #6	Action: Begin VP Character #2
	Section #7	Action: Lead's Subplot
3 VP CHARACTERS	Section #8	Action: Begin VP Character #3
	Section #9	Action: Lead Main Story Line
4 VP CHARACTERS	Section #10	Action: Begin VP Character #4
	Section #11	Action: Lead's Subplot
5 VP CHARACTERS	Section #12	Action: Begin VP Character #5
	Section #13	Action: Lead Main Story Line
6 VP CHARACTERS	Section #14	Action: Begin VP Character #6
	Section #15	Action: Lead's Subplot

Figure 9

#4, have your lead set a new section goal and take him through the phases as usual.

Six Guidelines for Juggling Story Lines

Depending on your novel's target length, you may or may not have more viewpoint characters' story lines to begin. Follow the pattern in Figure 9 to weave all of your novel's story lines, stopping when you reach the number of viewpoint characters in your novel.

Once you've begun all your story lines, keep in mind the following six guidelines as you continue plotting.

1. *Your lead will have more sections than any other viewpoint character.* Your novel is first and foremost the lead's story, and he will have far more sections than any of the other viewpoint characters. Among his sections, you'll distribute your other characters' sections.

The right-hand side of the NovelMaster in Figure 1 (page 59) tells you how many sections to use for each of your viewpoint characters. How you distribute them is up to you. Keep a running tally as you work so you'll know at a glance how many of each character's allotted sections you've used. For example:

	Gets	**Used So Far**
Jennifer (lead)	38	
Raoul (viewpoint character #2)	13	
Nell (viewpoint character #3)	13	

2. *Don't go too long without picking up any one story line.* Rotate your story lines so that you check in with all your viewpoint characters regularly.

3. *Always leave a viewpoint character other than the opposition on an action-section failure.* By leaving the reader hanging after a bad development, you're pulling her along wanting to see how that character will react. That's suspense.

4. *Remember that when you pick up a viewpoint character, he has not been in frozen suspension since the last section in which he appeared.* He has been performing action offstage that may or may not affect how he behaves onstage.

5. *Remember that a section in which a viewpoint character appears but is not the section character doesn't count as a section for that character.* You will undoubtedly have sections containing two of your viewpoint characters. Only one of them can be the section character, and you'll structure the section according to which one you choose.

6. *Use your judgment as to when to pick up the lead's main story line and when to pick up the lead's subplot.* There is no required number of sections for the lead's subplot, but don't

let it outweigh the main story line in importance. Pick it up frequently enough that the reader won't forget it and when it feels right in terms of how your story is developing. Most important, keep your lead's main story line and subplot separate—though feelings and thoughts from one will certainly flavor the other.

PLOTTING THE REST OF THE BEGINNING

Depending on the kind of novel you're writing, you'll have from ten to thirty sections in your beginning. If you're writing in the shortest word-length range—50,000–54,000 words—the pattern in Figure 9 will have taken you through section #7, and you'll have three more sections to plan to complete your beginning. If you're writing in the longest word-length range—150,000–154,000 words—the pattern will have taken you through section #15, and you'll have fifteen more sections to plan to complete your beginning.

By the end of the beginning, you should have introduced all of your characters in some way. Your viewpoint characters will have had their own sections. Other characters will have been present in some of these sections. If not, review your sections now and look for places where you can at least mention them. Since you're plotting, not yet writing, you could simply make a note such as "Thinks of Betty" or "Sees painting Josh did before the accident" or "Calls Edna to chat" or "Asks Clarissa, Larry's secretary, to put her through."

When you have only one section sheet left in your beginning, stop. We're going to do something special with that one.

To Recap
- Decide on your lead's subplot (romantic if there's a romantic involvement). Begin this subplot in section #4.
- Section #5 picks up the main story line from section #3.
- Use the "FROM" and "TO" guides on section sheets to track the flow of your various story lines.
- Use the NovelMaster (Figure 1, page 59) to determine the correct number of viewpoint characters for your novel. Designate your other viewpoint characters.

- Start your first (or only) story line centering on another character in section #6.
- In section #7, return to your lead's subplot.
- Refer to the NovelMaster for the number of sections to devote to each of your viewpoint characters. Keep a running tally as you plot.
- Always leave a story line other than the opposition's on a failure.
- Don't leave a story line hanging for too long.
- Make sure you've somehow introduced or mentioned all your characters by the end of your novel's beginning.
- When you've plotted the second-to-last section of your novel's beginning, stop.

Surprising the Reader

In This Step
- Story surprises
- A strong middle
- Plot patterns

For me, one of the most enjoyable aspects of reading a novel is being surprised. I love nothing more than to be shocked by a revelation or story development. I think most readers feel this way.

Surprises in a novel remind me that there's more to the story than I thought and that I'd better stay on my toes. A good surprise—one I never saw coming—makes me sit up and pay attention. Often these surprises come just at the moment when the story is starting to even out, when things need to be shaken up a little—or a lot.

That's no coincidence. Skillful writers know to place these surprises at strategic places in their novels to prevent the story from flagging or sagging or growing dull. I remind the writers I represent to make a point of inserting these shockers, though I am aware that the writers who plot their novels before writing them are able to make better use of this device. When you plan your story and can see the big picture, it's easier to determine what these surprises should be and to anticipate them by planting any necessary material earlier in the book. Writers who don't plot first—who make things up as they go along—must in effect surprise themselves at the same time they're surprising the reader. For these writers the shocker must come completely out of the blue; nearly always they must go back in the story and revise extensively to make provision for the surprise to come later.

With the Marshall Plan you're plotting your novel ahead of time and can tinker with your surprises till they're the best you can come up with. As for where to put them, that's easy:

Surprise #1 comes at the end of the beginning.
Surprise #2 comes at the exact middle of the novel.
Surprise #3 comes at the end of the middle.

WHAT'S IN A SURPRISE?

What, specifically, is a surprise? First of all, it occurs in an action section. To be precise, it's the failure in an action section, and as failures go, it's a doozy.

A surprise is a major, shocking story development that throws a whole new light on the lead's situation and makes matters worse in terms of her reaching her goal. A surprise can take the form of:

- A discovery your lead makes
- An action, by another character, that affects your lead
- Revelation of new information that is truly bad news for your lead
- An event that has a negative impact on your lead's situation

A surprise raises the stakes for the lead *and* makes the reader sit up and take notice. It always occurs as the failure of an action section, and always concerns the lead's main story line.

A surprise must be believable in light of what's happened in the story so far. It must also directly relate to the lead's pursuit of the story goal. Finally, the three surprises should get progressively worse.

Let's say your lead, Hank, has come to see his estranged wife to beg her not to divorce him. He argues that a divorce would be the worst thing in the world for their five-year-old son. At this point Hank's wife informs him the child isn't his. Surprise!

Let's try it for Sara's story. This will be an action section with no visible opposition. Sara has set a section goal of beginning to get her life back to some semblance of normalcy after convincing herself that, though Lance may be harboring secrets—perhaps of infidelity—being a member of the KKK isn't one of them. She's decided to let go of the whole issue, put it out of her mind, though there's no saying what the future holds for their marriage.

In the parking garage near the station where Sara parks her Jeep, she nears her car and is so preoccupied that she walks out in front of another car. Its driver swerves and hits Sara's Jeep, which explodes, killing the driver of the other car. Someone had planted a bomb in Sara's car. Surprise!

Make the last section of your beginning an action section and build in this kind of act-ending curtain—shocking, grabbing, dramatic.

A STORY IN PICTURES

Because a picture is worth a thousand words—or, in this case, anywhere from 50,000 to 154,000 words—Figure 10 is a diagram of how the sections in a novel's beginning might be arranged. This novel is 65,000 words long and has three viewpoint characters: the lead, the romantic involvement and the opposition. Alongside the diagram is the section tally as it would look so far. You may find it helpful to draw a diagram like this to track the flow of story lines in your novel's beginning, middle and end.

CRAFTING THE HEART OF THE STORY

An aspiring novelist once told me, "I'm great at coming up with beginnings and ends. It's the middles that kill me." Here was someone with not only a drawer full of false starts, but another drawer full of false finishes!

Many writers find the middle of the novel daunting. It does, after all, represent half the book's length, its action must pull the beginning and the end together into a viable whole, *and* it must not sag, drag or be boring.

The techniques presented in this step will help you construct a strong middle for your novel.

SECTION PATTERN IN A NOVEL'S BEGINNING

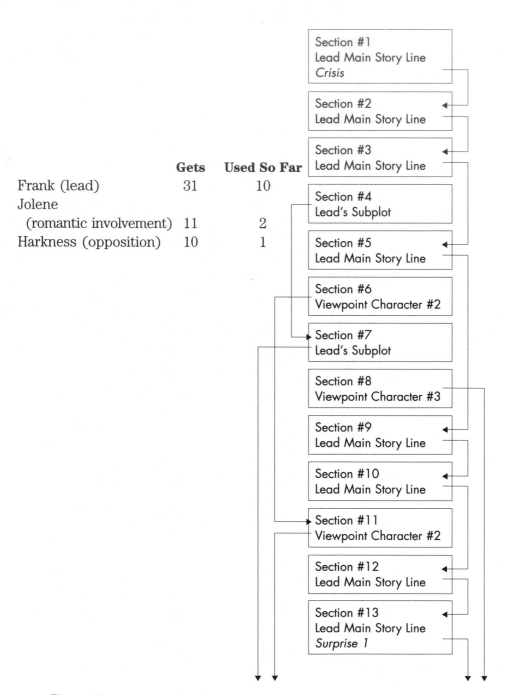

	Gets	**Used So Far**
Frank (lead)	31	10
Jolene		
(romantic involvement)	11	2
Harkness (opposition)	10	1

Section #1
Lead Main Story Line
Crisis

Section #2
Lead Main Story Line

Section #3
Lead Main Story Line

Section #4
Lead's Subplot

Section #5
Lead Main Story Line

Section #6
Viewpoint Character #2

Section #7
Lead's Subplot

Section #8
Viewpoint Character #3

Section #9
Lead Main Story Line

Section #10
Lead Main Story Line

Section #11
Viewpoint Character #2

Section #12
Lead Main Story Line

Section #13
Lead Main Story Line
Surprise 1

Figure 10

The Middle's First Sections

Refer to the NovelMaster in Figure 1 (page 59) for the correct number of sections for your novel's middle. Count out this number from your pile of section sheets and set aside the remaining sheets.

The first section of your novel's middle is a reaction section. It allows your lead to respond to the devastating failure of surprise #1.

Make your next section an action section for your lead. Here he springs into new action, getting the middle off to a lively start. The reader sees that even after being hit with surprise #1, your lead is up again and ready to fight.

In the third section of your middle, you can pick up either your lead's subplot or one of your other viewpoint characters' story lines, or you can stick with your lead's main story line if that feels right in terms of your story so far.

Continue weaving your story lines.

Worsening Failures

As you plot the middle, gradually increase the seriousness of your lead's failures. The worse the failures—the more dire the lead's situation—the more urgent it is that he attain his story goal. The stakes are rising for your lead. Options are narrowing.

Off on a Tangent

As in real life, your lead may have to follow some tangents in pursuit of the story goal.

Let's say you're writing a mystery in which your lead, the detective, experiences a failure where he learns that someone close to him, a person he never suspected, is somehow involved in the murder. In his next action section he seeks out Miss X, only to experience the failure of learning she's disappeared from her apartment. The sly landlady downstairs says she saw something important, but she won't talk without a good incentive. Your detective is broke, so in his next section he asks his brother to lend him some money. The brother does, but accuses your detective of coming to him only when he wants something, further straining their uneasy relationship.

Now that your lead has the money, he returns to the landlady and pays her. She reveals that she saw Miss X leave with a man—who had her at gunpoint. From the landlady's description of the man, your detective realizes he knows him—a sleazy local criminal. Your detective goes to the criminal's apartment and finds Miss X, only she's dead and the criminal's gone. Something about Miss X's body provides a clue which your detective jots down before anonymously tipping off the police about the body and then going in search of the criminal.

SURPRISE #2

Surprise #2 comes at the middle of your novel. Divide the total number of sections in your novel by two for the number of the section that will contain surprise #2. Write "Surprise #2" at the top of this section sheet.

When you reach this section in your plotting, make surprise #2 the failure in an action section for your lead's main story line, following the same guidelines as for surprise #1. It can be one of the same four options given for surprise #1 (see page 106).

Surprise #2 must be shocking but at the same time believable in terms of your story so far.

Surprise #2 must be worse than surprise #1. For example, surprise #1 might be the lead's discovery that a murderer has been gaining access to his victims' homes by impersonating the lead. In surprise #2, the lead could suffer a blackout and awaken in a pool of blood—a new victim's blood—and now he's not sure he's *not* the killer! Clearly surprise #2 is worse than surprise #1.

After the Surprise

The section after surprise #2 is a reaction section for your lead. Here he responds to the devastating failure and sets a new section goal.

Continue plotting.

SURPRISE #3

Surprise #3 occurs in the last section of your novel's middle, an action section for your lead's main story line.

Follow the guidelines for surprises, making surprise #3 the worst yet. It should be a failure so disastrous that it makes the lead's chances of achieving his story goal look virtually nil.

As you hit your lead with surprise #3, you're doing two important things: You're bringing down the curtain on your novel's middle, and you're setting the stage for your novel's end.

Follow the guidelines for surprises, making surprise #3 the worst yet. Keep in mind that your lead's reaction to this surprise will generate her final efforts to achieve the story goal. So make this surprise strong and dramatic and truly devastating.

We'll focus on those final goal-achieving efforts in step 8.

To Recap
- In the last section of your novel's beginning, plant surprise #1—a shocking development in your lead's main story line.
- Diagram the flow of story lines in your novel's beginning, if you think it will be helpful. (You can diagram the middle and end in this way, too.)
- Make the middle's first section a reaction section in which your lead responds to surprise #1.
- Make the middle's second section an action section in which your lead pursues the main story line.
- As you weave story lines in your novel's middle, worsen your lead's failures.
- Remember that it's OK to have your lead go off on plot tangents in pursuit of the story goal.
- Introduce surprise #2 at your novel's midpoint.
- Make the section following surprise #2 a reaction section for your lead.
- Insert surprise #3 in the last section of the middle.

Ending on All the Right Notes

In This Step
- Narrowing story options
- Ending story lines
- The Worst Failure
- The Point of Hopelessness
- The Saving Act
- The Wrap-Up

An editor once told me she was rejecting a manuscript I'd submitted to her, even though she'd loved reading it.

"Then why," I asked, "are you rejecting it? You just said you loved it."

"Yes, until the end. It fell flat and fizzled out. Darn it, when I stick with a book for four hundred pages, I deserve a terrific payoff!"

That's how you should view your novel's end, the last quarter of the story. It's the reader's reward for hanging in there. It's also what he'll remember most vividly about your novel, not just because it's the last part he'll read, but also because it packs more drama than any other part.

THE REST OF THE STORY

Your remaining section sheets represent your novel's end. To verify your correct number of remaining section sheets, refer to the NovelMaster in Figure 1, page 59. On the line for your word-length range, read across to the "Number of Sections" column headed "End."

Start the end's supercharged drama by making the first section a reaction section in which your lead responds to the devastating failure of surprise #3.

In the remaining sections of your novel's end, you'll be doing several different things at the same time. You'll be

- Narrowing the options and worsening the failures for your lead
- Resolving all story lines
- Tying up loose ends
- Taking your lead through the story points called Worst Failure, Point of Hopelessness, Saving Act, and Wrap-Up.

Figures 11 and 12 are patterns for juggling all these elements. Select one of the patterns according to whether your novel has a romantic involvement.

To use the pattern, begin by filling in the last number blank with the number of your last section. Then number the sections backwards until you reach the line for the number of viewpoint characters in your novel. Finally, go through the sections you've just numbered and copy onto the top of each one the notation from the pattern.

As you progress toward the end of your novel, your story lines resolve themselves and end. The less important the story line, the sooner it ends. The more important the story line, the longer you keep the reader in suspense wondering how it will end.

Your lead's main story line ends in your novel's second-to-last section. If you have a romantic involvement, that story line resolves in your very last section—proving that nothing's more important than love!

Anticipate having to tie up these various story lines and plot accordingly. It's OK to work backwards from where a story line resolves in order to figure out what will happen when. The goal is to arrive at the final, resolving sections naturally, to avoid cutting them off abruptly.

As for how the various story lines should end, sometimes you have a choice and sometimes you don't. See page 116 for a guide.

FINAL PATTERN OF SECTIONS—NO ROMANTIC INVOLVEMENT

6 VP CHARACTERS	Section # ____ Action: Lead's Subplot
↑	Section # ____ Action: Resolve VP #6 Story Line: *Goal Achieved* or *Not Achieved*
5 VP CHARACTERS	Section # ____ Action: Lead Main Story Line
↑	Section # ____ Action: Resolve VP #5 Story Line: *Goal Achieved* or *Not Achieved*
4 VP CHARACTERS	Section # ____ Action: Lead's Subplot
↑	Section # ____ Action: Resolve VP #4 Story Line: *Goal Achieved* or *Not Achieved*
3 VP CHARACTERS	Section # ____ Action: Lead Main Story Line
	Section # ____ Action: Confidant Story Line
2 VP CHARACTERS	Section # ____ Action: Resolve Lead's Subplot: *Goal Achieved* or *Not Achieved*
↑	Section # ____ Action: Opposition Story Line
	Section # ____ Action: Lead Main Story Line
	Section # ____ Action: Lead Main Story Line *Against Opposition: Worst Failure*
	Section # ____ Reaction: Lead Main Story Line *Point of Hopelessness*
	Section # ____ Action: Saving Act Resolve Lead Main Story Line: *Goal Achieved* Resolve Opposition Story Line: *Goal Not Achieved* Resolve Confidant Story Line: *Goal Achieved*
	Section # ____ Reaction: Lead Main Story Line: *Wrap-Up*

Figure 11

FINAL PATTERN OF SECTIONS—WITH ROMANTIC INVOLVEMENT

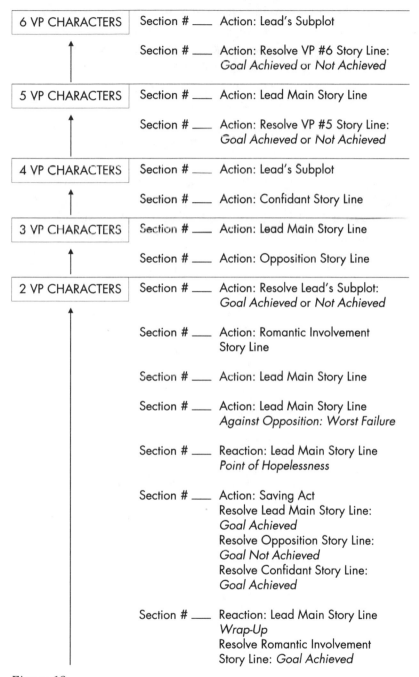

6 VP CHARACTERS Section # _____ Action: Lead's Subplot

Section # _____ Action: Resolve VP #6 Story Line:
Goal Achieved or *Not Achieved*

5 VP CHARACTERS Section # _____ Action: Lead Main Story Line

Section # _____ Action: Resolve VP #5 Story Line:
Goal Achieved or *Not Achieved*

4 VP CHARACTERS Section # _____ Action: Lead's Subplot

Section # _____ Action: Confidant Story Line

3 VP CHARACTERS Section # _____ Action: Lead Main Story Line

Section # _____ Action: Opposition Story Line

2 VP CHARACTERS Section # _____ Action: Resolve Lead's Subplot:
Goal Achieved or *Not Achieved*

Section # _____ Action: Romantic Involvement
Story Line

Section # _____ Action: Lead Main Story Line

Section # _____ Action: Lead Main Story Line
Against Opposition: Worst Failure

Section # _____ Reaction: Lead Main Story Line
Point of Hopelessness

Section # _____ Action: Saving Act
Resolve Lead Main Story Line:
Goal Achieved
Resolve Opposition Story Line:
Goal Not Achieved
Resolve Confidant Story Line:
Goal Achieved

Section # _____ Reaction: Lead Main Story Line
Wrap-Up
Resolve Romantic Involvement
Story Line: *Goal Achieved*

Figure 12

Character	*Story Line Resolution*
Lead's Main Story Line	In commercial fiction, the lead must always achieve the story goal. Readers want a happy ending; they want to see the character they've been rooting loudest for prevail—another of those payoffs. More to the point, editors like happy endings, too. So if you want to sell, make sure your story ends well!
Lead's Subplot (not with Romantic Involvement)	This one's up to you and depends on what your subplot is about. Use your instincts. Would the lead's failure to achieve the subplot goal add poignancy or an added touch of realism to your story? Or would your readers never forgive you? If a lead has just failed to achieve the subplot goal, achieving the story goal can have a bittersweet taste. Perhaps this would work for your story.
Romantic Involvement	The romantic involvement always winds up with the lead, which means the romantic involvement always achieves her story goal.
Opposition	Since the opposition's goal is to prevent the lead from achieving his story goal—and the lead always achieves his story goal—the opposition always fails to achieve his story goal.
Confidant	The confidant's story goal is to help the lead achieve the story goal. Since the lead always achieves his story goal, the confidant always achieves her story goal.

Additional	It's up to you whether your additional
Viewpoint	viewpoint characters will achieve their
Characters	story goals. It depends on what feels
	right for your story. You might use a
	combination of success and failure. One
	could even die.

NARROWING THE OPTIONS

As your novel's end progresses, give your lead fewer choices and fewer places to turn as she pursues the story goal. There are several ways of doing this.

Limit Success Routes

You can make it increasingly clear as the story progresses that the path to success lies in only one direction. Your lead knows this because he has already pursued other options, failed to find success and dismissed them.

Eliminate Characters

In addition to eliminating possible courses of action, you can eliminate *people*. Perhaps the classic illustration of this principle is the murder mystery in which suspects are killed off one by one. By the end, the detective's options in terms of apprehending the murderer are limited by virtue of fewer suspects being alive.

Rule Out Actions

You can narrow the options for your lead by having events occur in your failures that rule out certain courses of action. For example, you might have a lead who has always believed that if she could convince her father to forgive her brother, then the brother could finally come home and the lead could achieve her story goal of a happy, reunited family. But then, in one of your end sections, the lead is arguing violently with her father, who gets so upset he suffers a fatal heart attack. Now the idea of getting her father to forgive her brother is ruled out. The lead can no longer follow this path and must pursue other means of achieving her goal.

Use the Opposition

Have your opposition limit your lead's options. The opposition can work in the background, setting up obstacles in every road the lead tries to take. For example, your lead tries to convince a colleague to help him get a certain vital piece of information—but the opposition has reached the colleague first and won him to his side. Your lead attends an auction and bids on an antique desk that holds an important clue—but the opposition outbids your lead and wins the desk.

WORSENING THE FAILURES

One of your goals as a novelist is to keep your readers riveted to your book until the very end. The primary means of keeping them riveted is to keep them wondering whether the lead will achieve the story goal. Now, people are funny; they see only a quarter of the book left and think, subconsciously perhaps, "Not much story left; soon things will work out." After all, most commercial fiction does end happily, the lead finally prevailing. And knowing this, the reader relaxes a little, maybe doesn't flip those pages quite so fast.

You can't let that happen. Despite what a reader may intellectually know (that the book will end happily), you must keep her emotionally in serious doubt as to whether the lead will get what he's after. To do this you narrow the options, as discussed above, and worsen the failures.

At the beginning of your novel's end, your lead has just come off surprise #3, the worst setback yet. Don't let your reader—or your lead—off the hook by decreasing the magnitude of the failures. Keep things bad. The worse the situation becomes and the fewer the pages remaining, the more suspense you build—and that's better, more dramatic, more gripping reading.

So don't let up on your lead. Your novel's end contains few reaction sections. Action section follows action section in quick succession—failure after failure that increases your lead's desperation.

NO LOOSE ENDS

Inevitably, as you plot a novel, you will create situations that may remain unresolved when you reach your novel's end. I don't mean your various story lines; I mean smaller issues and questions that must be settled or resolved before the story is over so your readers don't say, "Hey, wait a minute. What about . . . ?"

Let's say Sara Bradford, in the course of her volunteer work at Helping Hand, meets a young woman with a sick baby. This woman is not a viewpoint character, but she's someone Sara sees repeatedly and is concerned about. She's background, in a sense. And yet by the end of the novel we'd better let the reader know that this baby is now under excellent medical care and will be fine, or that he's ill but there's hope if his mother keeps taking him to the hospital for treatment, or even perhaps that the baby has died—whatever makes the most sense in the story.

These threads aren't story lines and do not have their own sections. They are kept running within sections that have other primary functions, and you resolve them in action or reaction sections that have other primary functions.

A novel can have any number of such threads that must be tied. Did he get the scholarship? Did her mother ever return? Did that man down the street find his cat? Was the little boy from the house on the corner really stealing Sara's blueberries?

Resolve these issues, tie up these loose ends, before you reach the sections from the ending pattern. You'll have enough to deal with there without having to worry about these smaller matters. Also, you want your reader's mind clear of all worries except for how your various story lines turn out.

One last word on loose ends. When you tie one up, make sure any characters in your novel who should know how the thread tied up, do know. Otherwise, your reader's going to ask, "But does she *know* that? . . ." And that's a loose end in itself.

THE SECTIONS OF THE FINAL PATTERN

The pattern of sections that wrap up your novel's end is like the instructions the air traffic controller gives the pilot as he's landing the plane: The pilot has used his skills to navigate the bulk of the flight, but he needs some exact instructions to help him get the plane down exactly where he wants it.

You've used your plotting skills to get you this far; now I'm going to help bring your novel in for a perfect landing.

Follow these guidelines for constructing those all-important, keep-the-reader-riveted sections in the final pattern.

Lead Main Story Line or Subplot

The first of these sections will deal with either the lead's main story line or the lead's subplot, depending upon the length of your novel.

If your novel has from three to six viewpoint characters, this section will tune in on either of these story lines *in progress*. You're only a few sections from the resolution of either of these story lines, so increase the viewpoint character's desperation and hit him with a whopper of a failure.

If your novel has only two viewpoint characters, this section is the *resolution* of the lead's subplot, unless you have a romantic involvement. Increase the urgency for your lead, create a good strong conflict phase that keeps the question of the lead's success in the air for a while, and finish with either success or failure.

If you have a romantic involvement, do not resolve this subplot. End the section with a failure, as usual.

Additional Viewpoint Characters

These are the viewpoint characters other than your lead, romantic involvement, opposition and confidant.

The section in which you resolve a viewpoint character's story line is the last section from that character's viewpoint, but you don't have to remove this character from the stage entirely. You can have the character present in other characters' sections if that makes good story sense.

Confidant

If the confidant is one of your viewpoint characters, you'll have the section marked "Confidant Story Line." This is your last section from the confidant's viewpoint—though this is not necessarily the confidant's final appearance.

The confidant's story goal has been to help the lead achieve *his* goal. So, whether or not the lead is actually present in this section, show your confidant worried to death (just like your readers) that the lead will fail.

Since the confidant's story goal is directly tied to the lead's story goal, which won't be achieved till the end, we can't resolve the confidant's story line here. But we *can* have his section end on a failure, as usual, and this failure places the lead's success in even greater doubt.

Opposition

The section marked "Opposition Story Line" is the last section from the opposition's viewpoint—though it's by no means the last we'll see of him. This is your final chance to show him striving to achieve a section goal that will take him closer to his story goal—vanquishing the lead. Here, as always, the opposition's section ends on a success—which is bad for the lead and creates even further worry in the mind of your reader. The opposition has succeeded again; what hope does the lead have with so little time left?

Your lead may or may not be present in this section; go by your story sense. You could show the opposition in actual conflict with your lead, or you could show the opposition engaged in some activity that is harmful to your lead, perhaps a section with no opposing character.

Worst Failure

This is the big showdown, where the lead comes face-to-face with the opposition for the ultimate "battle." All other options have been closed off to the lead. Beating the opposition now is his only hope.

The nature of this showdown will vary greatly from one novel to another, depending on the nature of the book. A showdown is not necessarily violent or even physical. Not all novels' showdowns are confrontations at gunpoint on the roofs of skyscrapers. A showdown could be a climactic courtroom confrontation, a nerve-jangling chase sequence, a bloody fistfight, a rundown of the facts before the suspects (including the as-yet-unnamed opposition) or a quiet talk between your lead and her husband's mistress. It all depends on your story.

One requirement of the showdown is absolute: Both the lead and the opposition must be present.

This section is from your lead's viewpoint. Show him engaged in what should be one of the longest—if not *the* longest—conflict phase of all your action sections. Fill this conflict phase with lots of parries, lots of thrusts, lots of shifting of advantage between the lead and the opposition. Imagine your readers, like some surging audience at a boxing match, shouting, "Ooh!" and "Aah!" each time it appears that one, and then the other, will emerge victorious.

Then a terrible thing happens: Your lead suffers his *worst* failure of the entire novel. Does it appear—perhaps even to you—that there's no possible way your lead can overcome this failure and achieve his story goal? If so, that's good; your failure is severe enough. If not, make it worse!

This is the point where you want readers to say things like, "Oh my God, now what will he do?" or "She's through."

Point of Hopelessness

The Point of Hopelessness is a reaction section, and it's the darkest, bleakest reaction section in your novel. In it your lead responds to the Worst Failure. He truly believes at this moment that he has failed in his attempt to achieve the story goal and all hope is lost.

A reaction section may represent two days or two minutes. You must do what's right for your story.

Let's say you're writing a historical romance in which the lead learns at the end of the showdown that the romantic involvement—the lead has just told him her unborn child is his—won't have her because he's a man with a past and he'll never be good enough for her. Though we know he loves her, he treats her cruelly to push her away. The lead, her heart breaking, quickly packs her belongings and takes the next stagecoach out of town.

Her Point of Hopelessness occurs during her trip home. Alone on the stage as it crosses the dusty plains of West Texas, she has lots of time to react, first emotionally, to what has happened. How could he treat her so coldly? He must never have loved her in the first place. Were all her efforts, then, for nothing? She's been a fool, a fool with a broken heart and a baby on the way. She cries for the loss of a love she realizes she never really had.

Then comes the rational phase of the reaction section. Our heroine, calmer now, analyzes what happened between her and the romantic involvement. Even as she tries to make plans for her life back in Baltimore (she'll tutor privately and quietly raise her child, all she has left of the romantic involvement), she keeps remembering the look in his eyes when she told him she was expecting—first pure joy, then a darkening sadness.

Suddenly it all makes sense. He *does* love her. But when he learned of the baby, all his old fears returned, fears that he could never rise above his shadowy past and be the husband she deserves, the father their child deserves.

She won't let him go! He loves her as much as she loves him. She'll go back to him and make him see that she loves him for exactly who he is; he doesn't have to become anyone else to be a perfect husband and father.

This reaction section could take place over several days of solitary brooding and analyzing, and that's appropriate for this story.

Here's an example at the other extreme. You're writing a thriller in which the showdown has your lead facing the opposition, a serial killer, on a catwalk high above the floor of an abandoned factory. There is a bloody and extended struggle, during which the advantage shifts repeatedly between the two men. At one point the killer stabs the lead in the thigh; in agony, the lead pulls out the knife and pockets it. Then the lead realizes that the catwalk ends in midair and he's standing at the edge. The opposition, who sees this too, pulls back a heavy iron beam hanging from a chain and lets go. It swings into the lead, knocking him off the catwalk, but as he falls he grabs the edge and is now hanging by his hands. The killer, smiling, walks toward him.

Our lead's Point of Hopelessness occurs in about ten seconds. Emotional: He's been a fool; he's going to die; he's afraid; he worries for his wife's future. Rational: The killer is coming toward him. The killer is wearing running shoes, and the catwalk is made of steel mesh. Our lead remembers the killer's knife in his pocket. . . .

For this story, a ten-second Point of Hopelessness makes sense. In fact, anything else would be ludicrous. You'll know what's right for your story.

In both of the examples above, the lead had an insight or realization that enabled him to set a new goal. This insight or realization is important to your Point of Hopelessness. It will enable your lead to turn the entire story around in his favor.

When you devise this insight or realization, make sure it is believable and doesn't come out of the blue. You may have to go back to earlier sections of your story to plant "ammunition" for this insight.

For example, in the historical romance, we might have gone back and added the romantic involvement's statements about being afraid he'd never be good enough for her, that he'd always be a gunslinger. We might also have added that fleeting look of joy that appeared at the news of the baby, only to be quickly replaced by the look of sadness.

For the thriller, we might have had to go back to add the stabbing so the lead would have the knife.

If this ammunition is already in place in your story, so much the better. If it isn't, think carefully and plant what you need.

The Saving Act

At the end of the Point of Hopelessness the lead has set a new goal. In the next section, an action section, the Saving Act occurs.

The Saving Act is the lead's *execution* of the goal he set at the end of the Point of Hopelessness. It is our pregnant heroine facing the man she loves. It is our bleeding lead stabbing the killer.

The Saving Act always works. The lead does succeed in turning the story around, defeating the opposition, and *achieving the story goal*. Cross out "Failure" on the section sheet and replace it with "Success!" Then cross out "New Goal." Your lead needn't set any more goals, but one more section follows.

The Wrap-Up

If you have a romantic involvement, you haven't yet resolved the romantic story line (unless you're writing a romance, in which the romantic story line *is* the main story line). It's the only unresolved story line, and you keep it till the end—although the lead had a more pressing story goal, achieving that goal is empty and meaningless without the one he loves beside him.

Here, then, resolve your romantic story line, leaving the reader knowing the lead and the romantic involvement have gotten together or are sure to. Use whatever tactic is natural for your story. For example, flushed with emotion from having achieved the story goal, the lead rushes into the arms of the romantic involvement and kisses her. Or perhaps they take each other's hand or smile at each other knowingly. Not every romantic story line has to end with a tearful, passionate embrace.

In your Wrap-Up you must also have your lead do and/or say whatever would be appropriate after having achieved the story goal. But don't go on too long. Quickly tie up your story in this section, a coda to the Saving Act.

For example, if your lead has succeeded in rescuing his son from kidnappers and the son was wounded during the showdown, it would make sense for the lead to visit his son in the hospital in the Wrap-Up. Perhaps you'd want the entire section to take place at the hospital bed. Your lead and romantic involvement could hold hands as they gaze down at the poor exhausted child, who is sleeping peacefully.

Place. Your Wrap-Up can take place in exactly the same location where the Saving Act occurred, if that makes sense in your story.

Time. Your Wrap-Up can take place immediately after the Saving Act, or later that day or the next day, or a few days later—whatever works for your story. Sooner is better, though.

A COMPLETE ROUTE

You did it! You plotted an entire novel. You have your road map of your story from start to finish, and you'll never stall because you'll always know where you're going.

Now all you have to do is write it. That's next.

To Recap

- The end is the reader's reward, a strong dramatic payoff.
- Make the first section of the end a reaction section in which your lead responds to surprise #3.
- As you near the end, narrow the lead's options by limiting success routes, eliminating characters, ruling out actions and having the opposition close doors.
- Keep worsening the lead's failures.
- Tie up any loose ends before the final pattern of sections.
- The final pattern of sections (Figure 11 [page 114] or Figure 12 [page 115]) shows when to resolve your story lines; the guide beginning on page 116 discusses *how* you should resolve them.
- Complete the pattern sections, finishing with your lead's Worst Failure, Point of Hopelessness, Saving Act and finally, the Wrap-Up.

Part 3

How to Write Fiction Like a Pro

In This Part . . .

This part tells you how to write the story you've plotted.

Putting It All Together

In This Step
- Viewpoint writing
- Writing the action section
- Writing the reaction section
- Connectors

Congratulations. You know more about crafting a novel than many aspiring fiction writers, and you haven't even started writing the sections you've planned. Before you begin writing, you need a thorough understanding of a concept that will determine how you write those sections: viewpoint writing.

THE ART (AND CRAFT) OF VIEWPOINT WRITING

Every section of your novel focuses on a specific viewpoint character. Regardless of which other characters are in the section, the reader will be shown the feelings and thoughts of this viewpoint character only. The section itself will be written according to the perceptions and awareness of this character. That's viewpoint writing.

Many beginning novelists complain that when they're writing, they have no idea what to show and what not to show, what to describe and what not to describe. Viewpoint writing answers these questions.

Let's say you're writing a section in which the viewpoint character has entered a room he's never been in before. Naturally he would take in the room on entering, so you would describe the room *as he sees it*.

If, on the other hand, your viewpoint character enters a place he *has* been before, he wouldn't take mental note of how the place looks. But what if something in the place has changed? He would notice that, so you'd have him think about it. When you describe it, the reader knows that the details are coming to him through the perceptions of the viewpoint character.

The same concept applies to people. If your viewpoint character is sitting at her desk and her boss walks in, your viewpoint character isn't going to take in the details of the boss's appearance; she's seen him hundreds of times. But she might notice anything that's different—the boss's distinctive clothes or his windblown hair.

Conversely, if your viewpoint character meets someone for the first time, it's natural for him to take in the details of that person's appearance; we all do that when we meet someone. When you describe this character, the reader knows he's getting this description through the perceptions of the viewpoint character.

Describing Naturally

There's one problem with viewpoint writing. Although your viewpoint character may have seen her boss a hundred times, the reader hasn't, and the reader needs to know what he looks like. How do you show us what he looks like without writing a description that would be unrealistic for the viewpoint character to think about? There are two ways.

1. *Work with the change loophole.* Let's say the boss always wears the same five drab suits, but it makes sense in your story for him to be extra dressed up today. He's wearing a new silk vest with one of his old suits. So you use the vest as a natural excuse for your viewpoint character to think about how the boss is dressed.

2. *Work with details in action.* Let's say your viewpoint character has entered a New York delicatessen where she lunches nearly every day. Pick out a few details that make sense in your story, show what the place is like, and give the character an excuse to think about those things. An

old waiter with an overloaded tray yells, "Coming through!" when he's already practically on top of her. Your character has a friend, an elderly woman who works behind the counter, who winks at your character and compliments her on her new coat when she comes in.

Viewpoint as Filter

Viewpoint writing makes all the decisions for you. Your viewpoint character is walking in a garden and sees some purple flowers. Should you give their name? If the viewpoint character knows their name, yes. If not, no; you would simply write something like:

> Masses of purple trumpetlike flowers crowded over the edge of the path.

Your viewpoint character sees a bit of an old movie on TV and knows what she's seeing . . .

> On the TV they were showing *The Ghost and Mrs. Muir.* Gene Tierney was scolding Rex Harrison for scaring somebody away.

. . . or doesn't.

> On the tube they were showing some old flick. A pretty enough dark-haired actress with an overbite was scolding a man dressed like some kind of sea captain.

Viewpoint writing even determines how you say certain things. Since everything is filtered through your viewpoint character's consciousness, even what seems to be straight description is occurring through the perceptions of the character. So you might write any of the following passages, depending on the character who's registering it:

> On the TV they were showing some boring old black-and-white flick.

> On the TV they were showing one of those wonderfully romantic movies from the forties.

On the TV they were showing one of those corny old movies where just kissing was a big deal.

This concept also applies to writing in feelings/thoughts mode, in which we hear a character's distinctive inner "voice." Writing is filtered through the consciousness of that character; it should *sound* like that character.

Working With Awareness

When you use viewpoint writing, your reader knows only what the character knows or is aware of at any given moment. If you break from viewpoint writing by using devices like *little did he know, he could not know what was to come, he did not hear the ringing of the telephone* and *unbeknownst to her*, you shatter the illusion that we are experiencing your story through the character as it transpires. You remind us that this is, after all, just a made-up story and that you, the author, know what's going to happen.

Whenever you're in doubt about what or how much to show at any given point, turn the question over to viewpoint writing. It will guide you not only in instances such as those I've described, but also in countless others which will arise as you work.

Would you describe your viewpoint character's appearance? Viewpoint writing says you wouldn't do so from that character's viewpoint, unless the character would have a specific reason to think about his own appearance (but not the old looking-in-the-mirror or glancing-at-the-storefront-window chestnuts, please).

Would you write ". . . when Grayson, her family's trusted retainer, entered the room"? Viewpoint writing says no, because she wouldn't realistically think that. By Grayson's actions, we'll know he's the butler. You can show she trusts him by how she speaks to him.

Would you write "He got into his silver Jaguar and screeched away"? Again, viewpoint writing says no. To him it's just his car; he wouldn't realistically be thinking about its make or color. If it's important for readers to know it's a silver Jaguar, find another way to tell them. Use change or action; something another character says; something the viewpoint character *realistically* thinks, like "If old Clayton succeeded in getting him fired, he'd soon be driving a used Hyundai instead of this Jag."

Perceptions in Viewpoint

When you use viewpoint writing, readers know they are experiencing the story through the viewpoint character's perceptions. Therefore, when you describe acts of perception, the verbs of perception *saw*, *heard* and *smelled* are unnecessary. Simply describe the perception.

Instead of writing "He looked out at the street and saw a boy whiz past on a skateboard," write "He looked out at the street. A boy whizzed past on a skateboard."

Instead of writing "June stopped and listened. She heard leaves crunching behind her on the path," write "June stopped and listened. Leaves crunched behind her on the path."

Instead of writing "Dale sniffed. He smelled her perfume—the scent of azaleas—lingering in the air," write "Dale sniffed. Her perfume—the scent of azaleas—lingered in the air."

WRITING THE ACTION SECTION

How long should an action section be? Aim for five to six typed manuscript pages.

Work from your section sheet.

Where exactly should you start the action? If you take too long to get into the heart of the action—the conflict—your readers will become impatient. So tell just enough to set up the section. A few paragraphs at most should do it.

Unless the section runs directly from the previous section, indicate within the first paragraph

1. The section character.
2. The time (taken from "When" on the section sheet). If the section just before this one was about this same character, the time can be relative to that section:

   An hour later . . .

   That night . . .

   The next morning . . .

If the previous section was not about this character, state the time absolutely:

At two o'clock Friday afternoon . . .

Monday night . . .

On Sunday morning . . .

Stating the time of a section is one of those instances when you just say it—plainly, simply and soon—without trying to be artistic and imaginative. Readers don't want imaginative here; they just want their bearings before they dive into the good stuff.

3. The place (taken from "Where" on the section sheet).

Updating the Reader

Consider whether anything has happened to your character since his last section that the reader should know about. There might even be events that occurred just before the start of the section. Update the reader now, before the section action gets started.

It was after nine [time] when Jody [section character] pulled into the tiny lot next to Audrey's Bar and Grill [place]. Luckily, Mrs. Augustine downstairs had been willing to baby-sit Kevin, though she'd made Jody promise to be back by eleven [information].

What Jody had come to do wouldn't take that long. Audrey's was packed, but Randy wasn't hard to find. The bastard was in his usual spot by the rest rooms, hunched over a Budweiser. She'd better ask him for the money fast [statement of section goal] before he got too drunk, if he wasn't already. He got real mean when he was drunk.

As you begin the section, consider whether the reader has a clear understanding at this point of what the viewpoint character's section goal is. The reader may know it if, for example, this character's last section was a reaction section, where the goal would have been stated.

On the other hand, even if the viewpoint character's last section was a reaction section, if other sections have followed, you may have to remind the reader of the viewpoint character's section goal.

Or the goal may never have been stated. Even if it hasn't been stated, it may be implicit simply by virtue of the character's being here now.

If you have any doubt whether the reader will know what your character will be pursuing in this section, tell him. The reader must share the viewpoint character's goal.

Find a subtle or at least realistic way to convey the section goal. You can do so in feelings/thoughts mode, for example:

> She made an effort to calm herself, to smile. She'd never get Peter to agree to the new custody arrangement if she showed the slightest sign of hostility.

You can use dialogue in a perfectly straightforward way if it works in the section:

> "What the hell are *you* doing here?"
> Laura forced her smile to remain. "Peter, I . . . I want to talk to you. Please. It's about the custody arrangements. I've worked out something I think is fairer to us and to Timmy, and I want you to consider it."

Conflict and Failure

Get into your conflict as soon as you can. Milk it for all it's worth—lots of parries, lots of thrusts. You can start out quietly, if that makes sense, and build into a more heated exchange. Or you can rise immediately to battle pitch and stay there. Have your viewpoint character try several tacks but get nowhere in terms of achieving the section goal. Finally, when you've played out the conflict long enough that you feel you've exploited its full dramatic potential, move to the failure.

The failure must come crisply and dramatically; it can't be a halfhearted, wishy-washy no. It's a splash of cold water in your viewpoint character's face, a slap—wham!—like this:

Marguerite gazed deeply into his eyes and pressed herself hard against him. "Am I not what you've been looking for, m'lord?"

"Without question." Damon's voice was low, breathy.

He was hers now, she knew it. "Then why not take your prize?"

"Because I have already claimed another prize."

She drew back and looked at him.

He nodded simply. "Your sister Francesca. We are to be wed in May."

Once you've dropped the bomb, end the section as quickly as possible. Think of the failure as a second-act curtain in a play: Too many (or any) additional words or actions after the dramatic closing line could seriously weaken the impact.

Of course, often the failure bomb must consist of more than one line. Poor Marguerite could ask a pertinent question or two of Damon without robbing the section ending of any of its power. She could also briefly react.

"Francesca? But—you don't even *know* her."

"Know her! Who do you think was my Masked Goddess in the Via Veneto?"

She gasped. She opened her mouth to speak but nothing came out.

He was watching her, concern in his eyes.

She picked up her skirts and ran from the room.

WRITING THE REACTION SECTION

How long should a reaction section be? Aim for four to five typed manuscript pages.

Work from the section sheet.

Ground the reader in time and place (unless this section runs directly from the action section that caused the reaction).

Begin by restating the failure the character is reacting to. You can do this through dialogue, if the viewpoint character is with another character, or through feelings and thoughts.

Convey the emotional phase and the rational phase through either dialogue or feelings/thoughts. These two phases should form the bulk of the section. Depending on the seriousness of the preceding failure, play up the emotional phase. If it's appropriate—for example, in a murder mystery, where the lead does a lot of thinking—play up the rational phase.

Finish with the viewpoint character deciding on a new goal.

Showing Emotion

When you describe a character's emotion in a reaction section— or anywhere else in your novel—it's not enough simply to state the emotion: "She was furious" or "He was heartbroken." First of all, you'll have an awfully short emotional phase. But more importantly, it won't have much impact on the reader. That is what writing teachers mean when they talk about telling rather than showing. If you tell the reader Bob is disconsolate over the tragic drowning of his son, you have translated and labeled his emotional state for the reader. You have placed yourself between Bob and the reader, distancing her.

Let the reader see for herself that Bob is disconsolate. Let her see Bob doing what is in character for Bob to do when he's disconsolate. Review a character's fact list, if necessary, to get a feeling for how he might react emotionally to any given situation. But whatever the character might do, *show* him doing it. Does Bob wander through his day like a zombie, not hearing anyone at work? Does he sit in his son's room, hugging the boy's belongings? Does he burst out in a rage, smashing things? Does he do all or some combination of the above?

Show the reader, through a character's words and deeds. Don't expect her to believe you if you *tell* her. Emotion is as emotion does.

Time in the Reaction Section

Time is more flexible in a reaction section than in an action section. In an action section, summary is kept to a minimum and events are presented in detail as they happen. But in a reaction section you may, if it's appropriate to your story, show a character reacting over several hours, days, weeks, even months. To do so, use summary mode to show time passing— focusing, of course, on the emotional and rational phases of the section. In any reaction section, you're likely to have your viewpoint character's everyday life going on in the background. You'll undoubtedly do so if your reaction section covers a lot of time.

> Over the next week Mara went about her housework like a robot. Somewhere at the edges of her awareness, Robert and the girls hovered as if waiting for something—she had no idea what. They didn't push her, barely spoke to her, nor she to them.
>
> On Saturday morning she collected laundry from the hampers, took it all to the basement and began loading the washer. She stopped, holding up a T-shirt Bryan had loved, the one with Bart Simpson on it. She stuffed it against her face, smelling Bryan's sweet smell.
>
> And then she was on the floor, on her knees, crying so hard no sound came out, still clutching Bryan's shirt.

In the above passage, summary mode shows the swift passing of time, focusing on Mara's emotions by showing her moving zombielike through her days, the family nervously hovering. Then the passage shifts to action mode to focus on an incident and show it blow by blow. Switching between summary and action modes is an effective technique; in fact, you should always try to stop and spotlight an incident this way periodically during summary to bring the reader back from the distance summary creates.

CONNECTORS AND HOW TO USE THEM

Think of your novel's sections as pearls in a necklace. The best-made strands of pearls have tiny knots in the string between the pearls, to hold them tightly in place and keep the necklace strong.

In your novel, the knots between your pearls are called *connectors*. They're devices to connect your sections as effectively as possible.

The Space-Break Connector

Whenever a section featuring one viewpoint character is followed by a section featuring a *different* viewpoint character, use the space-break connector. When you reach the end of one section, simply hit Enter twice, creating a space of one blank line, and then begin your new section.

Rosamond gazed out the window of the taxi. Her house was gone. In its place stood a pile of charred, smoldering rubble.

[blank line]

At 3:30 on Friday afternoon Bernard found Kim sipping coffee in the student lounge.

Use the space-break connector after any action section when you want to heighten the dramatic impact of the failure.

Henderson spread out his hand on the table. "Five of a kind. The plantation is mine, Mr. Ashworth."

[blank line]

Edward Ashworth sat in his stateroom, unable to accept what had just happened, what he had just done.

You can also use the space-break connector to indicate the passage of time between two sections featuring the same viewpoint character. When you use the space-break connector this way, indicate at the end of the first section when and where the next section will take place. Then, when you start the new section, skip the time and place indicators.

"Fine," Benjamin said, "we'll just have that conversation— if you show up. Seven o'clock, the café at the Hilton."

[blank line]

The café was deserted except for a couple of tourists at the far end near the lobby entrance. Benjamin took a seat at the bar.

If a space-break connector falls at the beginning or end of a page, use a centered asterisk to indicate the break.

The Run-Together Connector

The run-together connector may be used between two sections featuring the same viewpoint character when neither a dramatic break nor any connecting text is necessary.

Here are two action sections with a run-together connector.

"David, I want to talk to you. Open the door."

"I told you, I'm not talking to anybody. Go away!" [end of first section]

Burt went to the living room and dialed Dr. Norris. The secretary put Burt right through.

Here are an action section and a reaction section with a run-together connector.

"You!"

Kyle spun around. Dennehy was staring straight at him, eyes on fire.

"What the hell are you doing here?"

"My job," Kyle answered.

Dennehy came up to him. "Your *job* was to keep your hot hands off Helen Holliston. You've proven you can't *do* your job."

"I told you—"

"Get out of my sight. You're off this case. And I want to see you in my office tomorrow, eight o'clock." [end of first section]

Kyle wandered through the dark back streets of Belston, vaguely aware that he was heading for his house. He clenched and unclenched his teeth until his jaw throbbed, and he kept pounding his fist into his hand. How could he have been so stupid?

And here's a reaction section followed by an action section, with a run-together connector:

. . . and shut the book with a bang. There was only one way to get the diamond back. She would steal it. [end of first section]

First thing in the morning she went to see Mrs. Speroni, the disguise expert Magda had told her about.

The Summary Connector

The summary connector can be used between two sections featuring the same viewpoint character. The summary connector is useful when a space-break connector is too dramatic or too much of an interruption, but the run-together connector would be too abrupt. The summary connector may also convey useful information. Write this connector in summary mode, and keep the text of the connector brief—ideally no more than a paragraph or two.

> Yolanda tugged at the last drawer of Donald's desk. It held fast. Locked. Damn. She yanked open the top drawer and fished around in the mess for a key.
>
> Someone knocked on the door.
>
> "Donald? Are you in there?" It was Adrienne.
>
> Silently Yolanda rose from behind the desk, made sure everything was as she'd found it, and slipped back out the side door of Donald's office. [end of first section]
>
> For the rest of the afternoon she stayed at her desk, working hard. At one point Adrienne asked her if she knew where Donald was, but Yolanda said she didn't and looked sorry. She left the office on the dot of five and took the subway to Dominique's apartment. [end of summary connector]
>
> Dominique looked shocked to see her.

As you write, indicate the position of your connectors, so you won't get confused later as to where your sections begin and end. Later, of course, you'll remove these notations.

With an understanding of viewpoint writing and how to write sections and connect them, you're almost ready to get into the actual writing of your novel. All you need now is an awareness of the five fiction-writing modes, the subjects of steps ten and eleven.

To Recap

- Each section of your novel is written from the distinctive viewpoint of that section's primary character.
- In viewpoint writing, show everything the viewpoint character would naturally know and perceive as the character would know and perceive it.

- When writing an action section, aim for five to six typed manuscript pages.
- Immediately indicate (if necessary) the section character, the time and the place.
- Fill the reader in on anything important that's happened to this character since we last saw him.
- Start the conflict as soon as you can.
- Bring in the failure crisply and end quickly thereafter.
- When writing a reaction section, aim for four to five typed manuscript pages.
- Indicate character, time and place as above.
- Restate the failure the character is reacting to.
- Play up the emotional or rational phase according to the situation.
- Use connectors (space-break, run-together, summary) between sections.

Mastering the Modes I: Action, Summary, Dialogue

In This Step
- Action mode
- Summary mode
- Dialogue mode

In my years as an editor, packager and agent, I've noticed that many beginning novelists aren't completely conscious of what they're writing. They do the oddest things in the oddest places. For example, I once received a manuscript in which the author went into a lengthy account of the lead's childhood just as his car was about to smash into a tree. The only explanation I could come up with was that the lead's life was flashing before his eyes!

The way to write successful, salable fiction is to know what you're doing and why at all times; then you won't accidentally do the wrong things in the wrong places. You build this awareness from the ground up, starting with a thorough knowledge of the five fiction-writing modes—the five types of writing of which all fiction is made—including what they do and when to use them.

ACTION MODE

Action is the mode fiction writers use simply to show what is happening at a given moment in the story. In action mode, you show events in strict chronological order as they occur, you use action/result writing, and you never summarize events. Every action is dramatized.

Chronological Order

In real life, things are always happening at the same time. It's a chaotic world. Not so in the fictional world. In the fictional world, things happen one at a time, and that's how you show them. This rule makes life a lot easier for novelists.

For example, in the real world a car could swerve on an icy road and a child in back could scream and his father at the wheel could swear and the tires could make a sickening spinning sound—all pretty much at the same time. But in your novel you'd force events into some sort of order.

> At that moment the car swerved wildly to the left. The wheels whirred sickeningly on the ice. Jerry swore and spun the steering wheel. In back, Barbara screamed. "Shut up!" Jerry shouted.

There is no simultaneity in the above passage. Even events that undoubtedly occurred at the same time, like the swerving of the car and the squealing of the tires, are presented in order, one at a time. This is how you should try to compose most, if not all, of your action writing. That means instead of writing, "She smiled, taking his hand," you'd write "She took his hand and smiled." Instead of writing "She screamed as the bullet tore into his chest," you'd write "The bullet tore into his chest. She screamed."

In action writing, the word *as* is your enemy. So are *while* and *at the same time that*. Beginners use these constructions a lot. They believe they should depict simultaneous events simultaneously, as if faithfully capturing the world exactly as it operates constitutes better writing. It doesn't. *In a novel, events occur one at a time.*

If two things actually do happen at the same time and it's important to show it, use *-ing*.

> She winked at him and, swinging her hips, sauntered from the room.

> Keeping the pheasant centered in the rifle's sights, he squeezed the trigger.

Action/Result Writing

In the above example "She screamed as the bullet tore into his chest," the writer would have us believe that these events occurred at the same time. Could we, then, have rewritten the sentence as "She screamed and the bullet tore into his chest"?

This is, of course, ridiculous because the two events, we realize, did not happen at the same time. Until the bullet tore into his chest, she had nothing to scream about. "The bullet tore into his chest" is the action. "She screamed" is the reaction.

Here's another example.

Lila ran to the window and looked out, seeing Fannie's dove gray limousine parked at the curb.

Instead of an *as*, this sentence has an *-ing*. The writer would have us believe that these two events occurred simultaneously. Could we, then, rewrite the sentence as:

Fannie's dove gray limousine was parked at the curb and Lila ran to the window and looked out.

What? It's ludicrous, of course. The two events did not happen at the same time. Lila would not have seen Fannie's limousine unless she'd looked out the window. So, to present the events one at a time and in their logical order:

Lila ran to the window and looked out. Fannie's dove gray limousine was parked at the curb.

No Summary

In action mode, you never summarize events. You would never write "At the party, she had a wonderful time." You would either show the action, event by event, if it is pertinent to your story or leave it out altogether.

SUMMARY MODE

In summary mode you report your story action in a condensed, narrative form. You tell the reader what happens rather than show it; there's no blow-by-blow description of events.

Summary mode has four primary uses.

To Connect Sections

As shown in step nine, summary can take us quickly from one section to another.

"And if the report isn't on my desk by five today, you're fired." [end of section]

George backed out of Mr. Bender's office and ran for the elevator. He lunched at McDougal's, taking his time, and was back at the office at 2:30. [end of summary connector]

At 2:35 there was a knock on his door. It was Maxine, Mr. Bender's secretary.

She looked sorry for him. "How's it coming, George?"

"It's not," he answered cheerfully. "It's not coming at all."

To Report Events

Some story events are important for the reader to know about but don't call for full-fledged action or reaction sections.

That afternoon, she shelved the rest of the books from her cart, helped Mrs. Curtis water the plants and started to take down the fifth-grade artwork. There was no way anyone could say she wasn't working.

To Telescope Time

Use summary mode to tell about events that occur habitually or over an extended period of time.

Every morning for the next two weeks he drove to work by way of the aqueduct, and every morning the strange blond girl was there, beside the road, as if waiting for him.

To Focus on Emotion Rather Than Action

With summary mode you can convey a character's emotional state (in a reaction section) over an extended period of time without focusing on the character's actions during that time.

Like an automaton she moved through her day at the college, wondering if anyone could tell that her heart was breaking.

Summary should be used sparingly. Because it is the opposite of direct action writing, it distances the reader. Books containing too much summary, not allowing the reader to be privy to enough actual action, leave readers feeling distant and uninvolved.

DIALOGUE MODE

Technically, dialogue could be considered part of action mode, but it has enough of its own rules that I think of it as a mode of its own.

Let's talk first about what dialogue should do.

Advance the Plot

Dialogue must progress your story. If you're in the conflict phase of an action section and two characters are arguing, the dialogue *is* the conflict and must carry the weight of the section. This means no unnecessary chitchat or repetition, both of which abound in real-life dialogue but don't occur in fiction—yet another way a novel is different, more orderly, than life.

For example, in real life we might hear:

"Hi, Larry."

"Hi, Doug, how's it goin'?"

"Mmm, not bad, real busy at work lately. You?"

"Same. How's Ellen?"

"OK. Her mother's sick. Nicki?"

"She's all right."

"Uh, listen, Larry, I wanted to ask you something. It's about the McCormacks' barbecue last Sunday. At the barbecue, did you notice anything funny?"

"Did I notice anything funny? How do you mean?"

"Oh, I don't know. I mean, um, when Grant sat down at our table, I noticed he had a beer in his hand and he put it down."

"Yeah?"

"Well, um, later—you know, after he got so sick and, you know, died—well, did you see the beer bottle?"

"No, why?"

"Because it wasn't there. It was gone."

In a novel we might boil it down to the following, still natural sounding but right to the point and considerably compressed:

"Hi, Larry. Got a minute?"

"Sure, Doug, what's up?"

"I've been meaning to talk to you about the barbecue last Sunday. You notice anything funny?"

"No, why?"

"I did. When Grant sat down he had a beer. After he got sick and they took him away, the bottle was gone."

Tight, pithy dialogue not only advances your plot, it also keeps it moving quickly. Slow, flabby dialogue makes for a slow, boring book. Watch for possibly unnecessary words like *yes*, *no* and *well* in your dialogue.

Dialogue also advances the plot by conveying information. Dialogue informs the reader and is also a primary means by which characters gain new information that furthers the story. As a result of Doug and Larry's exchange about poor Grant and his beer bottle, either Doug or Larry will undoubtedly act on the new clue that has just been conveyed.

Sound Natural

Dialogue must feel spontaneous. In the conversation between Doug and Larry we eliminated a lot of those *ums* and *wells*, but still tried to retain the natural sound of spoken English. This means

- Sometimes using contractions ("I've been meaning to talk to you.")
- Eliminating some words ("You notice anything funny?")
- Using some short sentences ("I did.")
- Not allowing a character to continue uninterrupted for too long (A good rule of thumb is a three-sentence limit.)

Some beginning writers, in an attempt to reproduce dialogue exactly as it sounds, take great pains to present dialect with all its idiosyncrasies. This is not a good idea. Readers inevitably trip on dialect.

"Lawd God, Serena, Ah done tole you ter git yosef away from dat winder 'fo this whole town knows yo' bidnez."

Instead of writing perfect dialect transcription, phonetic spellings and all, *suggest* dialect through word choice and arrangement.

"Well now, missy, I'd say your daddy and me are in for a mountain of trouble."

Create Distinctive Voices

Characters must not all sound the same. When you begin to write dialogue for a character, reread his character fact list, particularly his Distinctive Speech Pattern, to remind yourself of any special characteristics you have to work in. Even if a character has no character fact list, consider what sort of person he is and how he would likely sound. Strive for dialogue so distinctive the reader doesn't need any speaker identification.

"Julie, I'm concerned about your performance in my class."
"Oh God. I mean, like, what *is* the problem?"
"You haven't completed any of the homework assignments, and in class you are either disruptive or in another world. What do you have to say for yourself?"
"I'm, like, totally sorry, Mrs. Andrews."

Limit Tags

Dialogue should have a minimum of tags, or speaker attributions. Our improved Doug-Larry conversation contains no tags at all. We might have added "Larry asked" after "No, why?" just to keep things clear, but we certainly wouldn't have needed a tag after every piece of dialogue.

You should really only use tags to keep speakers straight. When you use them, stick almost exclusively to *said*, *asked* and *answered*. Many beginning novelists worry that repeated use of these words will become monotonous and unimaginative, so they search the thesaurus for *said* and *asked* replacements.

> "Don't you dare touch me," she hissed.
> "But I want you so bad," he husked.
> "Ooh," she thrilled, "I told you not to do that."

The fact is, *said*, *asked* and *answered* are invisible to readers. Look in any best-selling novel and you'll see what I mean.

When you use *said*, *asked* and *answered*, put the name first: "Bobbi said," "Trevor asked," "Bart answered." "Said Bobbi," "asked Trevor" and "answered Bart" are old-fashioned.

Often you can avoid *said*, *asked* and *answered* while still providing a tag by placing next to the line of dialogue a sentence whose subject is the speaker.

> "I'm afraid I have some bad news." Warren drew the letter from his pocket. "Marie left the country over a month ago."
> "Give me that." Yvonne grabbed the letter, scanned it. "I don't believe a word of it."

Minimize Gestures

Keep body language with dialogue to a minimum. Beginners often use gestures, mannerisms and other bits of "stage business" liberally in their dialogue. People are constantly smiling, grinning, nodding, shrugging, looking, eyebrow raising, head shaking and sighing. It's part of trying to deliver total realism.

In almost all cases these actions needn't be conveyed to the reader. First, there's nothing interesting about them; they add nothing to the dialogue. Second, many of the actions are rendered unnecessary by the dialogue. You needn't write:

> She shook her head. "No."

> Mary Ann shrugged. "I really don't know."

Always choose dialogue over body language, if you have a choice.

Sometimes an action within dialogue gives you a nice pause for introducing a new train of thought or adding drama. For example:

"I understand your pain, and you have my deepest sympathy. But I really have nothing to say." Adam gazed out to sea at a gull diving to the gold horizon. "Wait. There is something I can tell you about how Eleanor died."

Use F-A-D

Put feelings/thoughts, action and dialogue in the correct order. In the above example, the action—Adam gazing out at the gull—really cannot go anywhere else. It's while he's gazing that he decides to say more. Often you'll find that actions must go in specific places to provide beats or drama.

But there are other times when you do have a choice, and at these times you must follow the rules of action/reaction writing. Consider this:

"If you press that button, the entire Piroan Galaxy will be destroyed." A shiver of terror ran down Jeremy's spine. He stood perfectly still.

The passage reads strangely because the phases of feeling/thought, action and dialogue are not in the correct, logical order. Always remember F-A-D:

F eeling/thought
A ction
D ialogue

First comes the feeling or thought, which generates the action. Last comes the dialogue—how the character communicates his inner state to the outside world.

A shiver of terror ran down Jeremy's spine. He stood perfectly still. "If you press that button, the entire Piroan Galaxy will be destroyed."

Sometimes one of the F-A-D phases is not needed or is better left out; for example, when it's so obvious that it's understood to be there. If so, present the remaining phases in their proper order:

"Rhonda," Meg said sweetly, "I see you made your own gown."

Bitch. [No action shown] "That's right. Who did your hair, Meg? There's straw in it."

"Who the hell do you think you are, talking to my date that way?" Stuart said to Rhonda.

[No feeling shown] Rhonda pushed him hard in the chest. "Who do I think I am? I'm the girl you asked to the prom first!"

"Meg," Stuart said, "I'm sorry about what Rhonda said. She's just jealous."

He really was very sweet. Meg touched his smooth cheek. [No dialogue]

Break Up Exchanges

As with action, deliver "pieces" of dialogue one at a time for correct action/reaction. Consider the following:

"Have you ever been to Fiji before, Mr. Kramer? What kind of work do you do?"
"No, I haven't. I design outdoor shopping centers."

This, too, reads funny because the pieces are not broken up and delivered one at a time to be responded to separately.

"Have you ever been to Fiji before, Mr. Kramer?"
"No, I haven't."
"What kind of work do you do?"
"I design outdoor shopping centers."

Here's another mixed-up exchange.

Nausea rose in Nora's throat. She fell into the nearest chair and reached for Henry's handkerchief. "Henry, I'm going to be ill."
Henry handed her his handkerchief. "Just sit quietly, my dear, and you'll be fine."

In the first paragraph, two pieces are presented before the first can be responded to. The paragraph should be broken up, and the pieces of the exchange dealt with one at a time.

And the piece presented at the end of one paragraph should be responded to at the beginning of the next paragraph.

> Nausea rose in Nora's throat. She fell into the nearest deck chair and reached for Henry's handkerchief.
> Henry handed it to her.
> "Henry, I'm going to be ill."
> "Just sit quietly, my dear, and you'll be fine."

Paragraph Often

Begin a new paragraph for each new speaker. Readers expect a fresh paragraph to signify a change of speakers. Doing so is especially necessary when you have no dialogue tags: The paragraphing does the work for you. Even if a speaker has only one sentence, as Henry does above, or a single word of dialogue, move on to a new paragraph.

Minimize Adverbs

Keep adverbs in dialogue tags to a minimum. Another amateurism is the use of adverbs to describe how something is said. We've already gotten rid of the *hissed*s and the *husked*s, so I won't bother you with the likes of "she breathed languorously" or "he rasped contemptuously". But what about "she said languorously" or "he asked contemptuously?" They're bad form. In the best writing, the words of the dialogue themselves convey how they are spoken. If you find that it's not clear from the dialogue how it is spoken, you can rewrite the dialogue. For example:

> "How would I know?" she asked angrily.

could become

> "How the hell should I know?"

or

> "How on earth would I know?"

If the way a character says something is truly important, give it its own description.

Lord Fitzhenry pulled off his gloves a finger at a time. "I think, Lady Varick, you'll find your daughter already quite disposed to becoming my wife." His voice was like warm honey.

"Ha! You call yourself a man." Her voice was pure contempt.

Sometimes you simply have to use a *said* replacement or an adverb after a dialogue tag because there is no other way to convey how the words are said . . .

"Quick, come to my room," she whispered.

. . . or when the words would usually be spoken in a completely different way.

"I hate you so much," she said lovingly.

If you describe how a line of dialogue is spoken, do so *after* the dialogue. We can't know how something is said until it's said.

Use Correct Dialogue Punctuation

Follow the specialized rules of punctuation in dialogue. Dialogue should reflect actual spoken English as closely as possible. Toward that end, punctuation in dialogue today is kept simpler, less formal, than in other writing. Don't use any colons or semicolons within dialogue. In regular narrative you might write:

I'll tell you this: She's never seeing Timmy again.

But in dialogue you'd write:

"I'll tell you this. She's never seeing Timmy again."

or perhaps:

"I'll tell you this—she's never seeing Timmy again."

In regular narrative you might write:

Vanessa was no angel; she was a sadistic, calculating woman.

But in dialogue you'd write:

"Vanessa was no angel. She was a sadistic, calculating woman."

To show interrupted or sharply broken-off speech, use a dash.

"And what did David say he was going to do on that—"
   "Objection!"

Punctuate a line of dialogue interrupted by an action like this:

"When I grow up"—he spread his thin arms wide—"I want to be as fat as Uncle Louie!"

To show speech that trails off, use an ellipsis—three periods with one space before and after each.

"If you don't come out of that closet this instant, I'll . . . Darn it, come out at once!"

For added realism, try this trick once in a while: Place the name of the person being addressed, set off by commas, between two separate but related complete sentences.

"You're no gentleman, Lord Fitzhenry, you're a thrill-seeking womanizer."

Spell out numbers in dialogue.

"She'll be here at six-thirty."

"I took a cab to Forty-fifth Street."

For dates and other long numbers it is acceptable to use numerals.

"Weren't you born on November tenth, 1951?"

"The serial number on the VCR is 6239416."

Summarize Sometimes

Know when to summarize dialogue. Summarized dialogue, or indirect dialogue, is almost always a bad idea. New writers often lapse into it for no apparent reason.

And then he told her he loved her, that he had always loved her, and that if she didn't say she'd be his forever, he just didn't know what he might do.

Clearly this summary of dialogue distances the reader by putting the writer between the reader and the story to sum things up. You don't ever want to distance your reader.

The above example would be better presented in direct dialogue. But there are times when summarized dialogue is the correct choice.

When the Exact Words Don't Matter. Sometimes a character explains something that the reader needn't see in its exact words because the explanation itself is not important to the story.

"And this is the laundry room." Tina led the way in. "Washer, dryer." [Summarized dialogue:] She explained how to use both machines.

When Dialogue is Mundane. Sometimes a character says something so routine that we don't need the exact words. For example, when characters order in a restaurant:

Mary Lou threw her napkin onto her lap. "If he calls me sweetheart one more time, I'm reporting him to Human Resources."

"You should have done that two months ago."

The waiter appeared and [Summarized dialogue:] they ordered salads.

Mary Lou waited until he was gone. "I don't know, maybe I shouldn't have had that affair with him."

Or when characters begin and end a telephone conversation (skip the *hellos* and *good-byes*):

Jake leaned back on the sofa and switched on an old western.

The phone rang.

It was Allen. "Come on. It's time."

"Now? I thought we weren't doing it till tomorrow."

"She left early. What do you want from me?"

"OK, I'll be at your place in twenty minutes."

Jake switched off the TV and hurried to his bedroom to change.

When the Reader Already Knows. Sometimes a character tells another character something the reader has already read about.

"Mom, I've got something to tell you. It's about Linda."

"Linda? She's home? You saw her?"

[Summarized dialogue:] As gently as he could, he told her what Dr. Jordan had said in his telegram.

His mother looked at him, her face expressionless. Then her eyes rolled back in her head and she sank to the floor.

Action, summary and dialogue are the most dynamic of the five fiction-writing modes. Most of your story's actual events occur in them.

In step eleven we'll discuss the two remaining modes, feelings/thoughts and background.

To Recap

- In fiction writing, always be aware of what you're doing and why.
- Action mode shows events in strict chronological order, using action/reaction writing with no summary.
- Summary mode can connect sections (when a summary connector is appropriate), report events whose details aren't important to the story, telescope time, and focus on emotion rather than action.
- Dialogue must advance your story, sound natural and distinguish characters. Limit tags, minimize gestures, use F-A-D, break up exchanges, paragraph often, minimize adverbs in tags, use correct dialogue punctuation and summarize when appropriate.

Mastering the Modes II: Feelings/Thoughts and Background

In This Step
- Feelings/thoughts mode
- Background mode

The two modes we'll discuss in this step are *informing* modes; they convey information vital to understanding what's going on in the story. These modes are static—they don't move the story forward. You never want your story to stay in one place for too long. On the other hand, without these modes the reader would be utterly confused. So a skillful writer uses them judiciously—only as much as is absolutely necessary, and in the correct places.

FEELINGS/THOUGHTS MODE

Feelings/thoughts mode is often used in small pieces along with dialogue. But this mode can be used more extensively on its own to show the workings of your viewpoint character's mind.

The conveying of feelings and thoughts in novels has been made unnecessarily complicated. The preferred way (preferred by editors and readers, that is) is simply to state the thought, either indirectly (the preferred method) or directly.

You rarely need tags like "she thought" or "he wondered," which viewpoint writing (discussed in step eight) renders unnecessary, and which also distance the reader.

Compare this example of indirect thought:

Ian walked to the edge of the platform and looked down the tracks. When would the train arrive? he wondered.

to this one:

Ian walked to the edge of the platform and looked down the tracks. When would the train arrive?

It's clear he's wondering. The same principle applies to direct thought.

Compare:

Lorna smiled coyly. "I've had a boyfriend or two."
  Or two hundred, he thought. "Oh, I don't doubt that!"

to:

Lorna smiled coyly. "I've had a boyfriend or two."
  Or two hundred. "Oh, I don't doubt that!"

Don't use italics or quotation marks for thoughts. However, if a character is recalling dialogue, put the recalled dialogue in italics.

Roger stopped in front of Claire's town house. There was a big pinecone wreath on the door. Dana's tricycle sat beside the walk. That meant they were home.
  He touched the present on the passenger seat, looked again at her house. Would she turn him away? *This is it, Roger. I don't want to see you again. I mean it.*
  He looked once more at her door, shook his head and pulled back into traffic.

You'll no doubt use the largest blocks of feelings/thoughts writing in the emotional and rational phases of your reaction sections—especially if the character is alone. Here it becomes obvious that one "he thought" or "she wondered" after another would be intrusive and unnecessary. Simply state—indirectly or directly—the feelings and thoughts.

He dropped to the floor and leaned against the damp cinder-block wall, his heart thudding. His arm still burned where that—that *thing* had touched him.
  He had to get out of here, quickly before it tried to get in again. But *how*? There were no windows, only the door,

and *it* was behind the door. He could scream for help, but would anyone hear him through eight inches of concrete?

No, there was only one way out.

BACKGROUND MODE

Background mode is exactly what it sounds like: providing the reader with factual background information. Like feelings/thoughts mode, it must be used sparingly and in the right places.

In every novel some background is necessary, but it's inherently boring because it necessitates stopping the current story—something you want to avoid. Beginning writers give far too much background, then compound this mistake by putting the background where it shouldn't go.

> She put down the phone and gazed about her desk at the lavish office. She'd been with Turner, Wade & Roche for four years now, having joined the firm as a partner after leaving Hollis & Sloan, a smaller firm in Hartford. Before that she'd gone to Fordham Law School, and previous to that. . . .

All wrong. And so boring. We might as well read her resumé. A reader's instinctive reaction to straight, undigested background like this is the same as her reaction to gobs of straight description: She wants to skip it, even if she knows it might be important to the story. So keep background to the barest minimum in your novel: Boil it down or convert it to other modes or stamp it out entirely.

Give Background as Explanation

Provide background only when something has come up that needs explaining. This rule makes life so easy for you. You explain only what's important to understand the story at this moment.

Let's say your lead, a museum curator, walks into a cluttered antique shop and sees, lying dusty and ignored in a box of assorted junk, a certain Japanese vase she's been seeking all her professional life. Now, without some explanation, her next actions won't make sense to the reader. So we explain now, at the point that she sees the vase. Notice that we present the explanation as dialogue, so it's not straight, ordinary background.

Kendra made her way down the narrow aisle between rows of stacked boxes. It all looked like a bunch of junk—hardly what she'd have called antiques—beneath a thick, gray blanket of dust.

A familiar shape among the jumble in one of the cartons made her stop. It appeared to be a vase, about eight inches high, narrow at the bottom and flared at the top, like the petals of a lily.

No, it couldn't possibly be, not in a million years. She laughed at the notion. She picked up the vase and blew on it. Dust flew everywhere, but the vase was still hidden by a thin coating of grime. She took a tissue from her purse and rubbed at the vase. A vivid pattern emerged—cobalt and cherry and black lines against a background of deep yellow.

Her heart pounded. She kept rubbing.

"What on earth are you doing?" Jerry had come up behind her.

She turned to him.

"Kendra, you're white as a sheet. What's wrong?"

She held the vase in front of him.

At first he frowned in puzzlement. Then his brow drew back and his eyes widened. "You're not saying—"

"Jerry, it is."

"But you told me the last of the Yamaguchi vases had been destroyed."

"I thought they had."

"You said you'd looked everywhere."

"I thought I had." She rubbed her thumb on the vase's deeply glazed surface. "I was twenty-three when I held one of these. It belonged to my father. Then it was stolen and he offered a reward—a million dollars."

"A million! You never told me anything about that. Is that what it's worth?"

Her gaze lowered. "Not to poor Daddy. He doesn't even know who I am anymore. But to some people it's worth much, much more."

Minimize Background

You needn't tell readers all the background on a character's fact list. Indeed, you're unlikely ever to do so. You created that background to help you bring the character to life. If you must give some of it to the reader to explain something in the current story, fine; but don't give it just for the sake of giving it—a common beginner's mistake.

Even when you've decided that some background is called for, scrutinize it to make sure the reader really needs *all* of it. She probably doesn't. Boil it down to the absolutely essential facts. Remember, straight background is the enemy.

Not only should you present it briefly; you should also present it just once. Give your reader credit for being able to remember what you've told her—or to flip back through your book to re-read a bit of background if necessary. You can, of course, allude to a piece of information you've already presented.

Jerry remembered what Kendra had said about the reward her father had offered for the vase.

Withhold Information

Understand that readers needn't know every detail of a character's background before they can follow that character's present story and give him their sympathy. New writers often write pages and pages of a character's background early in a novel. They erroneously believe that readers shouldn't be asked to follow the story of a character, or to care about a character, whose entire life story they don't know. The opposite is true. You should deliberately withhold background until the reader really needs it. In fact, the longer you can hold back the juiciest, most important background information, the better.

Break It Up

Don't present too much background at one time. Spoon-feed it to the reader so she is barely aware she's getting it. It's like poison: A minuscule amount every day is harmless, but a lot at once is fatal. Small doses of one or two sentences work best.

Convert to Other Modes

Whenever possible, convert straight background into action, dialogue or feelings/thoughts mode, or a combination of these. The above passage about Kendra and the vase is an example of background presented in dialogue mode.

Let's say your novel's lead is raising her twelve-year-old son alone because her husband walked out on them a year ago. Instead of just telling the reader this through flat, undramatic, straight background explanation, you could present it through a combination of action, dialogue and feelings/thoughts mode, like this:

> Cheryl tapped on Donnie's door and opened it slightly. He sat on his bed, his legs crossed, his head in his hands.
>
> "Donnie? What's wrong?"
>
> He looked up. His eyes were red. He held out a light-blue piece of paper.
>
> She took it. Across the top were the words "Twin Rivers Annual Father-Son Camping Trip."
>
> She smoothed his hair. "I'm sorry, honey. I'm sure it hurts a lot."
>
> Suddenly he slammed his fist down on the bed. "I hate him, I hate him! Why did he have to leave? Doesn't he care about us? I'm supposed to have a father."
>
> Her eyes filled and she swallowed down a growing lump. "Yes, you are. I'm as angry as you are. But Daddy couldn't cope with being a father . . . or a husband. So maybe it's best he left."

Be careful when you use dialogue to convey background information that you don't lapse into the kind of stagey, artificial dialogue that is convenient to write but doesn't reflect how the characters would really speak. Simply ask yourself, "Would this person really say this? Is he volunteering too much?" If there's something a character must say, work the conversation so he would naturally say it.

Use a Flashback When Appropriate

If you absolutely must show a past event exactly as it occurred, put it in the form of a flashback. There's a lot of controversy about the flashback. More than any other device, it brings your story to a complete halt and asks the reader for much patience. If you must use a flashback, reward the reader's patience by writing the flashback in a dynamic form: Structure it as an action section, complete with failure.

Here's an example. A young woman named Carlotta agrees to a blind date. When he walks in, she recognizes him immediately as a man with whom she had a highly sensual anonymous encounter at a friend's garden party two weeks ago. We want to show that encounter exactly as it took place.

> Edwina giggled. "He's coming. He's so handsome I'm tempted to take him as *my* escort."
>
> Jonathan looked appalled. "Edwina!"
>
> "Oh, calm down, Jonathan, I'm not nearly pretty enough for him. Shhh, here he comes."
>
> He stepped into the doorway.
>
> Carlotta's breath caught in her throat.
>
> It was him. She could never mistake the sardonic turn of his full lips, the perfect straightness of his nose, those black, black eyes. Hadn't she been drawn to him because of those very features, a man she didn't even know?
>
> It had been only two weeks ago. She was standing in the middle of the lawn at Harrowhill, the estate of the actress Gloria Gladstone, who was giving the party in honor of her cousin, just returned from Australia.
>
> "Carlotta," Gloria said, "allow me to introduce my cousin, Josiah Bland."
>
> He was a short, fat man with sparse pale hair. He bowed and kissed Carlotta's hand.
>
> Then she saw *him*. Standing by the orchestra tent. Watching her. She tried to take her eyes off him but couldn't, even as with a lift of one brow and a tilt of his head toward the house, he indicated that she should meet him inside.

"Carlotta, are you quite all right?"

"I feel a bit light-headed." What was she doing?

He had turned and gone up the sweeping stairs into the house.

"I . . . must go inside for a moment."

Her head really was spinning as she lifted the skirts of her gown and climbed the stairs.

The hall was dim and cool. He was nowhere about.

A soft cough came from the room on her left. She entered it, a small parlor.

"Do you do things like this often?"

She jumped. He stood only inches away.

"No, I . . ."

He took her hand and drew her into the shadows at the far end of the room. He pulled her close, and she felt his warm breath on her neck. He kissed her there, so softly, and then his lips were on hers. She thought to fight him but the impulse fled, and she was lost in him, this man who, three minutes ago, she'd never seen. When at last their lips parted, she leaned back and looked at him.

He was smiling. "I believe you *do* do things like this often."

Hot blood rushed to her face. She turned and ran, his soft laugh pursuing her.

She had run from the house. Unwilling to encounter anyone, she had hurried around to the front, summoned her carriage, and demanded to be driven home.

He was watching her now, but this time he wasn't smiling.

"Carlotta!" Edwina whispered. "You're being frightfully rude."

A present-story cue (his features) sets up the flashback. Two *had*s take us into the flashback, which is written in the simple past tense. Two more *had*s take us out of the flashback and back to the present story.

Never use a flashback too early in your novel. Wait until after the first three sections.

Keep the flashback as brief as possible; trim it to its most pertinent action. If it must run on for more than a couple of pages, split it into two or more flashbacks, bringing us back to the present story in between.

If you use a flashback in an action section, wait for a relatively quiet moment. Don't stop dramatic action or dialogue to present a flashback.

Keep It Up Front

Get all background out of the way by the end of your novel's beginning. The beginning is where you set everything up; readers bear with you as you introduce all your characters and provide all necessary background information. But the middle and end of your novel should be concerned exclusively with the present story. Readers will have little patience for background presented this late, when the story has really picked up speed.

BE MODE AWARE

When you write, be conscious of what mode you're in at any given time. That way you won't accidentally slip into the wrong mode at the wrong time. Eventually, switching among the modes will become second nature to you.

To Recap
- In feelings/thoughts mode, state thoughts and feelings indirectly or directly.
- Use background mode only when the reader will be confused without it.
- Present only the vital facts, and present them only once.
- Withhold the most interesting material as long as you can.
- Break up background into small pieces.
- Convert background to other modes to maintain reader interest.
- Use a flashback if absolutely necessary.
- Confine background to your novel's beginning.

Completing a Draft

In This Step
- Your writing work space
- Your writing schedule
- A writing plan
- Goals and rewards
- Manuscript format

You're ready to write.

To not only start your novel but finish it, you need a disciplined plan. This plan must address *where* you'll write, *when* you'll write and *how* you'll write. If you can stay focused on these three aspects of writing at all times, you'll have the process licked.

THE NOVELIST'S WORK SPACE

Where will you write? Your work space is important because it will affect how you feel, which will affect how you write. You want a place where you'll feel creative and comfortable, a place that encourages you to produce your best work.

Your work space needn't be fancy, but it should be a place that is permanently yours and won't be disturbed or invaded by family members. Using the kitchen or dining room table is a bad idea because you'll be forever setting up or packing up. (Besides which, if you'll write on a desktop computer, you'll want to set it up somewhere and leave it there.)

An actual office in your home is great, but so is an alcove or a bedroom corner or even a basement corner, as long as you don't find it depressing. Your work space should be a cheerful place.

Now make sure you've got plenty of room for working. Begin with your computer, dedicated word processor, or typewriter and a desk or table large enough to accommodate it and still provide space to spread out your notes, character fact lists, section sheets and research materials.

Pay special attention to the height of your work surfaces. A writing surface should be thirty inches off the floor, but a keyboard should be only twenty-six inches. This is why a desk return, which is usually lower than the main portion of the desk and is designed for this purpose, is a good idea if you have room. There are also keyboard supports that can be mounted underneath a standard desk so both your writing and keyboarding surfaces are the correct height.

Along with your computer or word processor you'll need a printer. Laser, ink-jet, *letter-quality* dot matrix and daisy wheel printers are all acceptable. No nine-pin dot matrix printing, the bane of every agent and editor (and our ophthalmologists).

You need a solid, comfortable chair with adequate support for the base of your spine and a backrest high enough for you to relax against (it should come to at least the lower part of your shoulder blades). The chair should also have arms.

Make sure you have enough light. If there's not enough overhead, supplement with a quality desk lamp to cast light on your work surface.

File drawers are helpful but not mandatory. Your desk may have a file drawer or two, or you can set up a small freestanding file unit beside your desk or table if you have room. In your file drawers you can store ideas, research notes, clippings, manuscripts, copies of submission letters and other correspondence—and, eventually, your book contracts.

Also extremely helpful is a bookcase, or at least a shelf, for your reference books. Some writers like to keep these books right on their desk within easy reach, between bookends. You might want to consider doing that if you have room.

A bulletin board is useful if you have the wall space nearby. You can buy the traditional cork variety or the magnetic kind you can write on with dry markers. On this bulletin board you can post your characters' photo sheets and fact lists. The board is also handy for displaying inspirational items, such as a letter from an agent or editor asking to see your material.

Once you start sending material, you'll want a wall calendar to track it. Treat yourself to a calendar with illustrations you like, and hang it near your desk or table.

Now you can outfit your space with supplies. First you'll need plenty of paper. For your drafts any kind will do: ruled white or yellow pads, plain white copier paper, even newsprint. I would advise against using paper bound into spiral notebooks; you'll want to be able to shift pages around easily. I also think using the back of used paper, though ecologically correct, is a mistake because the writing or printing on the used side can become confusing or distracting. For final manuscripts, buy *white* (never any other color) 20-pound (74gsm) bond with 25 percent rag or cotton content.

Next, gather other supplies:

- Your choice of pens, pencils and markers
- If you use wood pencils: a pencil sharpener—manual or electric
- If you use mechanical pencils: extra lead
- Erasers
- Extra ribbons, ink or toner for your typewriter or printer
- If you use a computer or word processor: blank diskettes
- If you use a typewriter: correction fluid, cleaner for the keys
- A stapler with lots of extra staples
- Paper clips—regular and jumbo
- Butterfly clamps
- Binder clips (small, medium and large)
- Rubber bands
- Transparent tape
- Plain white business-size (#10) envelopes
- Large (9″ × 12″ [22.9cm × 30.5cm] and 10″ × 13″ [25.4cm × 33cm]) kraft clasp envelopes

- Large (12½″ × 17½″ [31.8cm × 44.5cm]) plastic-padded mailers
- Blank mailing labels
- A postage scale
- A letter opener
- Self-stick removable notes
- A ruler
- A quality pair of scissors
- A wastebasket
- If you have a file drawer: hanging file folders with tabs and plastic holders; manila folders to use within the hanging folders
- If you have a cork bulletin board: pushpins
- If you have a magnetic board: your choice of dry markers, magnets
- A clock—wall or desktop
- A calculator (to tally your royalties!)

Store items you'll use often close at hand, in drawers or in containers on your desk. Supplies you'll use less frequently, such as envelopes and extra printer cartridges, can go in closets or cabinets.

Don't forget personal items that will make your writing work space a more pleasant place to be. Add pictures of family or friends or pets, or a favorite knickknack. And don't forget to display reminders of any previous writing accomplishments, such as a published story or article.

Make a decision about the telephone. If you need to be able to answer the phone no matter what you're doing, consider having a phone extension on your desk. If you like having a phone handy but want to be able to screen calls, think about using an answering machine. I like the digital kind (no tape mechanism to break); if you select this type of machine, make sure it holds enough message minutes. Some hold only ten minutes—not much if you're letting the machine take the calls for any extended period. If you can, buy a machine that lets you record two different announcements—one for normal times and one to switch on when you're writing. ("Hello, this is Margie. I'm writing from noon to three and can't take your call, but if you leave a message I'll call you back as soon as I can.")

Subscribing to a caller ID service can further reduce phone distractions. For many incoming calls you can see who's calling without having to listen to the answering machine.

While we're on the subject of outside stimuli, consider whether you like to have music playing while you work. I need absolute tomblike silence when I write, but I have worked with enough writers who can't work *without* their Debussy or Enya or easy listening that I make this suggestion to you. If you like music while you work, decide whether you'd prefer a simple desktop radio, a tape player or a full stereo system. You can even let your computer play your favorite CDs if it has a CD-ROM drive.

SETTING UP A WRITING SCHEDULE

There's no one correct writing schedule. The correct schedule is the one that works for you, which means you'll stick with it. Whether it suits you to write every day, only on weekends or only at night, the secret is to remain rigidly faithful to the routine you've set for yourself. Of course, sometimes life intrudes and a writing session is missed; when that happens simply return to your schedule as soon as you can.

To begin planning an ideal writing schedule, consider first the other demands on your time. Obviously, if you work a full-time job outside your home, your possible writing times are already limited to your off hours. But you have demands on your time at home, too, so you must think about your daily routine and pinpoint those hours when your time is truly your own, when you won't be disturbed or summoned. Be honest with yourself and identify those times, however scarce, when it would be feasible for you to write.

Perhaps your best time is very early in the morning (you could set your alarm an hour or even two hours earlier), before anyone else wakes up. Maybe it's at night, when everyone else is in bed. For one of the writers I represent, it's 10:00 P.M. to 5:00 A.M.; she then sleeps till noon. Perhaps your best time is after dinner, when everyone else is doing homework or watching TV. Or perhaps you have no free time during the week and must confine your writing to weekends.

The right time is when you can sit quietly to work *and* when you have the energy to do so.

When you have determined your ideal writing time, you must do three important things.

1. *Announce to your family, friends and anyone else who should know that you are embarking on a writing project and have set aside this particular time for this work.* Make it clear that you are excited about this project and it's extremely important to you. For this reason you are off-limits during these times, except for true emergencies—and state what these are. Listen to objections and counter each one calmly and rationally. "But you always make my school lunch then!" "Yes, but I'll be making it earlier in the day from now on." "But we always watch TV together at those times." "I know, and I'll miss doing that with you, but this is more important to me than TV, and I'll make a point of being with you more at other times." And so on.

2. *On your wall calendar, and in any datebook you carry with you, mark off your writing times for the rest of the year.* For example, on every weekday note "6-10 WRITING." Now promise that you will honor these appointments with yourself as conscientiously as you honor appointments with your doctor or dentist. That means that if you're setting up an appointment or meeting, these times are unavailable. Except for emergencies (for example, a sick child), make no exceptions.

3. *Show up!* At the appointed time, sit down at your desk and get to work. Forget anything else that might need doing— cleaning the house or vetting that contract or mowing the lawn or folding the laundry or reading that mystery you bought the other day. It'll all wait. If you find yourself obsessing over these other activities, tell yourself that you are just looking for excuses not to write and force yourself to stay at your desk and attend to your work. Even at your desk it's easy to find distractions— computer games, that other CD you want to hear, to-do lists for the rest of the week, that call you were supposed to make about soccer. If you find yourself doing any of these things, stop and

shake yourself; say aloud to yourself, "This time is for writing only!"

If you use an answering machine—and you really should—switch on message 2 (if you have one) during these times. Unless you must listen to calls—for instance, in case it's your child's school nurse—turn down the volume on the machine *all the way*. Don't screen the calls; screening implies you'll take some of them—and you're not going to.

READY, SET, WRITE!

OK, I'm here, it's quiet, my desk is stocked. Now what do I do?

Place your stack of section sheets in the center of your desk toward the back. Next to them, place your character fact lists. If you haven't already, tape your photo sheets to the wall (or post them on your bulletin board) where you can see them without turning.

Now, take section sheet #1 from your pile of section sheets. You'll be focusing only on this. From your stack of character facts lists, take the list for your lead, the viewpoint character of section #1. Reread the character fact list. Study the lead's photo sheet. Then reread section sheet #1. Now, on your computer or typewriter or legal pad (or whatever suits you), begin translating your section sheet into an actual section.

Keep this book handy on your desk and feel free to reread any parts necessary to remind yourself about a method or technique. For example, to write this section you might want to refer to "Writing the Action Section" on page 132.

I recommend that you devote a minimum of four writing sessions (of at least two hours each) to the writing of each section—at least when you're getting started with the plan.

When you've completed a section, print it out, if you're writing on a computer or word processor. Set it in its own pile so you can refer to it easily.

Each time you begin a new section, consider your options in terms of connectors, reviewing that part of this book if necessary (pages 137-140). Insert the connector you deem appropriate between the last section you wrote and the one you're now beginning.

Should you jump around when writing sections, perhaps starting with one in the middle of the novel that especially excites you? No! A novel, by nature, builds on itself. You'll be carrying thoughts and emotions and information from earlier sections into later ones. It should be impossible to write a section in the middle—in a vacuum, as it were—without writing preceding sections first. Always write your sections in order from first to last.

ON GOALS AND QUOTAS

I'm a firm believer in goals and rewards. Writing is a solitary occupation. There's usually no one around to reward you when you reach a milestone, yet those rewards are important. So give them to yourself!

Make completing a section a mini-milestone and do something nice for yourself: Take a leisurely bath, rent a video you've been wanting to see, make a recipe you love. When you do this nice something for yourself, make a point of being aware that you are doing it because of your writing achievement. Tell yourself you're doing well.

Should you share your accomplishments with family and friends? Do so at your own risk. I wouldn't. They love you but they won't "get it." Their responses may well disappoint you, so why not let it be your happy secret? If someone asks how the writing is going, just say, "Great! I'm very pleased," and leave it at that.

Larger milestones are completing your novel's beginning and middle. When you reach these, you deserve a gift. Why not buy yourself something meaningful in terms of your writing, like a reference book, a beautiful pen, a novel by a writer you admire? Of course, what you give yourself is up to you, but I always feel writing-related rewards bring a special pleasure. And each time you use them, you're reminded of what you accomplished.

The biggest milestone of all is, of course, finishing your novel. Major achievements call for major rewards. What's your pleasure? Dinner with your spouse, significant other or friend at that fancy place downtown? (*Now* you can talk about your writing.) A night away? That laser printer you've been eyeing? It's up to you—just make it really special.

You'll notice I've talked about reaching milestones but not about setting a timetable for reaching them. I don't believe in timetables or quotas; they're self-defeating. You've set a schedule, remained as faithful to it as possible, worked as hard as you could—why set dates when you have no idea how long a particular section is going to take you to write? If you set dates for reaching milestones and don't make those dates, you'll just feel bad about yourself. That's unfair—especially when the dates were arbitrary anyway. Do you really need that? I don't think so. This is supposed to be fun.

So, milestones and rewards—yes. Quotas and timetables and deadlines—no.

THE CREATIVE FLOW

As you're writing, don't worry about some point of grammar or spelling you're unsure about. You're in creative mode; you can worry about those mechanical issues later. Put a little question mark next to the part you're unsure about as a reminder to check it later.

Take your time with your writing. More important than writing fast is writing well. If you find yourself on a creative roll, go with it, but be prepared at other times to go slowly, laboriously. This is how most fiction gets written—a few pages a session. I know you're in a hurry to finish your novel and get it out into the marketplace. But agents and editors will wait. We'll always gladly wait for a wonderful novel.

What about those times when you sit down for your session and you just don't want to write? If you absolutely can't bring yourself to go forward, go back: Reread what you've written so far. You may find yourself getting back into the spirit. If not, reread your character fact lists. If you still can't write, force yourself to make some notes about how you'll translate the next portion of section sheet into text. Try to stay at your desk for your session's entire allotted time. Chances are you'll get back into the swing of things before the end, but if you don't, call it a day and figure things will go better next time. Just make sure you come back.

THE PROFESSIONAL MANUSCRIPT

Eventually, you'll finish your first draft, and though you'll edit and revise, you'll need to start putting your manuscript into proper professional form for submission to agents and editors. Follow these instructions. (Note that here we're dealing only with text; we'll cover the title page and chapter openers a little later.)

Set your left, right and bottom margins at 1¼" (3.2cm). Set your top margin at ½" (1.3cm).

Double-space all text.

Number your pages consecutively, from first manuscript page to last, in the upper right-hand corner of the page, against the top and right margins. Do not use *Page* or any hyphens or periods with the page numbers.

In the upper left-hand corner of every page, against the top and left margins, type a "slugline": your last name in uppercase and lowercase letters, a slash, then your novel's title in capital letters. The top of every page of your manuscript should look like this:

Smith/FAMILY AFFAIRS   36

The first line of text on each page should be about ¾" (1.9cm) below the slugline and page number.

Use courier type (on your computer or word processor, the point size 12) for *everything*. Never use boldface or actual italics. Indicate italics by underlining. Use no other fonts or typefaces, no decorative symbols—nothing!

Justify your left margin only. Your right margin is, as they say in publishing, "ragged," or uneven. Do not break and hyphenate words at the end of text lines.

Always indent paragraphs. Use an indention of five spaces. Never insert extra lines between paragraphs (except as space-break connectors).

Type two spaces after a period, a colon, a question mark or an exclamation point.

Type one space after a comma, a semicolon or a quotation mark.

Indicate a dash by typing two hyphens together. Do not leave any space before or after the dash. Just type "word--word."

Commas go inside quotation marks, like this: "Don't touch me," he said.

Type ellipses as three periods with one space before and after each, like this: But if Joanne wasn't at the bar that night . . .

Use single quotation marks only if you need quotation marks within quotation marks, like this: "Mother always said, 'If you can't say anything nice, come and sit by me.' "

When you print your final manuscript, use the 20-pound (74gsm) bond paper with 25 percent rag content. Always use black print only. Use only one side of the paper.

Do not bind your manuscript pages in any way, not even by chapter with paper clips. Stack the pages loose in a manuscript box (available at office-supply stores) or the box your typing paper came in. That's how agents and editors like to receive manuscripts.

That's it. If I haven't mentioned it, don't do it.

When your draft is finished and formatted—and you've rewarded yourself for reaching the big milestone—print out the full manuscript on draft paper (not the final-draft paper yet) and put it away for at least a few days. You need some distance from it now, because in the next part you'll put on the editor's hat and switch into analytical mode. You'll need to be as objective as possible about your own work to really make it shine.

To Recap
- Create a comfortable, permanent, well-stocked work space.
- Set a regular, realistic writing schedule and adhere to it rigidly.
- Keep section sheets, character fact lists, photo sheets and other materials at hand for easy reference.
- As you write your sections, refer to the methods and techniques in this book when necessary.
- Supply appropriate connectors between sections.
- When you reach milestones, reward yourself.
- Follow proper manuscript format.

Part 4

Polishing Your Manuscript

In This Part . . .

This part presents techniques for revising and editing your manuscript.

How to Be Your Own Editor

In This Step
- Checking story sense
- Strengthening your writing

Congratulations again. You have every right to be extremely proud of yourself. You have *completed* the manuscript of your novel.

REVISING AND EDITING

The hardest part is over. Your manuscript undoubtedly needs some revision or editing—all first drafts do, whether the author is brand new or a brand name—but you have your story down, start to finish. You have something to work with.

Now it's time to be your own editor. Cast as cold an eye as possible on what you've created, recognize its strengths and weaknesses, and revise and edit to bring the manuscript to its full potential.

Using the manual that follows as your guide, go through your manuscript as many times as necessary, looking for places that need improvement. Use a pencil in case you want to make further changes. Edit by simply crossing out words and writing in the line space above. If necessary, insert material on new pages.

I always advise against revising or editing directly on the computer. Text on the screen looks different somehow from text on paper. More to the point, we're more apt to miss errors or weaknesses on the screen. So print out and work with a hard copy—words on paper, the way your readers will see your work.

The advice in the checklists that follow will serve you well for every novel you write. Most of it will eventually become habit.

THE NOVELIST'S MANUAL FOR SELF-EDITING
Story Sense and Logic

✔ Does time track correctly in your story? Make a table showing when sections take place—"Monday 3:00, Georgette meets Dr. Anton"—paying special attention to the chronological relationship of story lines to one another. Make sure you've given characters enough time to get from one place to another. Adjust times as necessary.

✔ Are your characters' action-section goals always clear, whether stated or implicit? The reader must always know exactly what a character is going after. On the other hand, do you state a goal when the character's actions make it perfectly clear? Do the goals make sense?

✔ In reaction sections, are characters' emotional and rational reactions to failures logical? Believable? In character?

✔ Do characters' reactions to one another make sense in light of what has already transpired among them? Do you have them refer to previous events or interactions when it would be natural for them to do so?

✔ Are characters behaving logically in light of what has already happened to them? In light of what they know?

Describing Action

✔ Use adverbs sparingly. Delete unnecessary ones, and certainly delete strings of them. Often an adverb is trying to strengthen a weak verb: "Carla went quickly down the aisle." Instead choose the perfect verb that needs no strengtheners: "Carla hurried down the aisle." Mark Twain called the adverb the enemy of the verb.

✔ If you decide to use an adverb, use only one, and put it in the right place. For full effect and if possible, put the adverb at the beginning or end of the sentence: "Forlornly she waved at the departing train," or "She waved at the departing train forlornly."

✔ Delete unnecessary details. You needn't tell the reader that your character opened the cupboard, took out a can of beans, opened the drawer, took out the can opener and opened the can of beans. Just say "She opened a can of beans." If the reader knows the mechanics of an action, skip the details.

✔ Have you written in speaking language that would come naturally to your viewpoint character? If a character would say, "I went down the street to get cigarettes," you can write "He went down the street to get cigarettes."

Describing People, Places and Things

✔ Use adjectives sparingly—one at a time, never a string of them—if at all. Often an adjective is strengthening a weak noun. Choose a more accurate noun. Not "a light wind," but "a breeze." Voltaire called the adjective the enemy of the noun. (He should have gotten together with Mark Twain.)

✔ Know that *very* is one of the weakest adjectives. In almost all cases you can strengthen a sentence by removing *very*.

✔ Scrutinize every description. Is it too long? Do we need it at all?

✔ Be specific. Not just a dog, but a collie or a toy poodle or whatever it is.

✔ Spare us the weather reports. Beginners write a lot of them, thinking novels need them (Snoopy's "It was a dark and stormy night"). But they're boring. We've all experienced almost every possible kind of weather. Just tell us it's sunny or the sky is gray or there's a wet wind and get on with the story.

✔ Don't use a simile or a metaphor unless it would occur to the viewpoint character through whom you're writing; otherwise you as the author are intruding, shattering viewpoint writing. If it would occur to Arthur that the slime on the monster was like lumpy motor oil, fine.

✔ Whenever possible, focus on details, which add realism like nothing else. Don't just write "The subway station was shabby." Write: "Near the edge of the platform, a man with knotted hair held out a Dixie cup to no one in particular, calling, 'Spare some change? Spare some change?' Swirls of iridescent orange graffiti covered the Canal Street sign. The whole place smelled of urine and potato chips."

✔ Don't describe what doesn't need describing. We all know what certain things look like. Describe an object only if it differs from what we'd expect.

✔ Remember that in viewpoint writing, descriptions filter through the character. Not only should characters see objects differently, but one character might notice objects others wouldn't.

✔ Use the five senses when you can, though not all at once. Characters don't just see and hear; they feel, smell and taste, too.

✔ Whenever possible, give us description in action, not just static reporting. Not "At the water's edge stood a row of six tall flagpoles flying the flags of the six Piroan emirates," but "At the water's edge the flags of the six Piroan emirates billowed and snapped in the wind."

✔ Think of walk-on characters (the cab driver, the waiter, the bank teller) as furniture. They don't need describing unless doing so would evoke the setting.

✔ Describe only what's essential to what's happening. If a character walks down a hallway, we probably don't need a description of the wallpaper.

✔ Write in the positive. Tell us what was, not what wasn't. Don't write "There was no light in the closet." Write "The closet was dark." Don't write "She was not impressed with his repertoire." Write "She was unimpressed with his repertoire." Don't write "I will not allow you to see that man again." Write "I forbid you to see that man again."

Simplicity and Economy

✔ Delete redundancies. *Past* history. The sky *above*. Continued *on*. Hung *down*. The ceiling/roof *overhead*. A *cold* chill. He stood/climbed/rose *up*. He sat/slowed *down*. Join *together*. A *little* baby. A *brief* glance. She whispered *softly*. *Tall* skyscrapers. The *end* result. To find them you must closely scrutinize your writing. Better yet, choose your words so carefully that you don't use redundancies in the first place.

✔ Often you can delete unnecessary possessives, as in "She held up the diamond, her eyes gleaming." Write "She held up the diamond, eyes gleaming."

✔ Often you can delete *that*. Not "Emily knew that the clinic opened at eight," but "Emily knew the clinic opened at eight."

✔ Clean out qualifiers like *a bit*, *a little*, *fairly*, *highly*, *just*, *kind of*, *mostly*, *pretty*, *quite*, *rather*, *really*, *slightly*, *so*, *somewhat*, *sort of*. Like *very*, they're all weakeners, almost always unnecessary. Not "She just couldn't see the difference," but "She couldn't see the difference." Not "You really shouldn't say such things," but "You shouldn't say such things."

✔ Cut unnecessary articles (*a/an*, *the*) for stronger impact. Not "A sadness washed over her," but "Sadness washed over her." Not "The cars whizzed by on the freeway," but "Cars whizzed by on the freeway."

✔ Delete *and* at the beginning of a sentence.

Not:

"You better believe it," Elise said. And she gave him a slow wink.

But:

"You better believe it," Elise said. She gave him a slow wink.

✔ Often you can cut *of*. Change "students of the college" to "college students"; "members of the club" to "club members."

✔ Don't use *the fact that*. Not "The fact that Professor Jones was sick made it impossible for Emma to ask him her questions," but "Because Professor Jones was sick, Emma couldn't ask him her questions."

✔ Watch for circumlocution—saying things in an indirect or roundabout way. Not "The situation was nearing the point where they'd have to come out," but "They'd have to come out soon."

✔ Cut unnecessary words. Not "The smile on his face," but "His smile." Not "His heart thumped in his chest," but "His heart thumped." Not "He made his hands into fists," but "He made fists." Not "The fingers of his hand," but "His fingers."

✔ Watch for autonomous body parts: "His mouth/lips curved into a smile." "Her hand waved." "His arm rested on the back of her seat." "Her foot rubbed his under the table." Never have body parts act on their own, except for the eyes: "His eyes widened." Otherwise have the *person* act: "He smiled." "She waved." "He rested his arm on the back of her seat." "She rubbed his foot with hers under the table."

✔ When describing acts of looking, use *gaze* rather than *eyes* to avoid unintentional hilarity. Not "His eyes traveled around the room," but "His gaze traveled around the room." Not "His eyes dropped to the newspaper on the table," but "His gaze dropped to the newspaper on the table."

✔ Cut *began to* or *started* to unless you're describing a character truly starting a task or activity. Not "She began to laugh," but "She laughed."

✔ Don't overuse *then*. Remember: In fiction everything's consecutive; readers *expect* one thing to come after the other. Often you can use *and* instead of *then*, or start a new sentence. Not "Wendy crossed the terrace, then descended the wooden stairs to the beach," but "Wendy crossed the terrace and descended the wooden stairs to the beach."

✔ Don't tell us something twice. If a character is going to voice a thought, we needn't hear her think it, too.

Not:

Where in heaven's name could Johnny be? Greta wrung her hands. "Where is he?"

But:

Greta wrung her hands. "Where in heaven's name can Johnny be?"

✔ Don't tell us more than we need to know. Not "He threw her over his left shoulder, wrapped his left arm around her legs, and placed his right hand on her backside," but "He threw her over his shoulder."

✔ To avoid confusion, refer to each of your characters the same way every time.

Not:

"I've looked over your loan application," Mr. Abernathy said.
Lyssa twirled her wedding band. "Do we get it?"
The banker pinched the bridge of his nose. "No."

But:

"I've looked over your loan application," Mr. Abernathy said.
Lyssa twirled her wedding band. "Do we get it?"
Mr. Abernathy pinched the bridge of his nose. "No."

✔ Have you overused characters' names? If you're writing a section containing only a male character and a female character, use the names once at the beginning and then switch to *he* and *she*, perhaps using their names occasionally. If your section contains more characters and you must differentiate them using their names, you can still use a character's name at the beginning of a paragraph about him, then switch to either *he* or *she*.

Clarity and Precision

✔ Seek and destroy clichés: *hardy mums*, *butter-soft leather*, *a mighty oak*, *a trusted servant*.

✔ To show habitual action, use the past tense rather than *would*. Not "Each morning he would walk to the Y and swim twenty laps," but "Each morning he walked to the Y and swam twenty laps."

✔ Watch *it*, which should replace the noun that immediately precedes it. Not "He took an apple from the refrigerator and ate it," but "He rummaged in the refrigerator, found an apple and ate it."

✔ Don't use the weakeners *appeared to* or *seemed to*. Not "The road appeared to waver in the intense heat," but "The road wavered in the intense heat." Not "Her face in the portrait seemed to call to him," but "Her face in the portrait called to him."

✔ Don't tell us what you're showing us.

Not:

Teddy smashed his fist into the oatmeal.
Annoyed, Barbara shut her eyes and groaned.

But:

Teddy smashed his fist into the oatmeal.
Barbara shut her eyes and groaned.

✔ Limit the use of *there was* and *there were*. Not "There were ants all over the cake," but "Ants covered the cake." Not "In the next block there was the barking of a dog," but "In the next block a dog barked."

Grammar, Usage and Style

✔ Watch for and remove inadvertent rhyme.

✔ Don't use the same "important" word twice on the same page.

He gave her a *wary* look. "How long have you known Lance?"
"Four years." *Warily* she slid the papers toward him.

On the other hand, don't be afraid to repeat "unimportant" words.

Not:

She poured herself some coffee and carried it to her desk. Sipping the steaming brown liquid, she flipped through the report.

But:

She poured herself some coffee and carried it to her desk. Sipping the coffee, she flipped through the report.

✔ Watch for misplaced modifiers. "She lay on the bed beside him" has a different meaning than "She lay beside him on the bed." "The blue-eyed farmer's son" and "the farmer's blue-eyed son" are not necessarily the same person.

✔ Watch for introductory participles that don't modify the subject of the sentence—an error that slips past many editors. "Leaving the village, the mountains glowed red in the sun." "Opening the closet door, the cat sprang from the shadows." These statements give the mountains and the cat undue credit.

✔ Don't use *hopefully*, as in "Hopefully we'll win the lottery." Write "I hope we win the lottery."

✔ Watch for "Morse code"—too many dots and dashes in dialogue, favored by beginners. Do you really need so many unfinished sentences trailing off in ellipses? Probably not. Complete as many of these sentences as you can. Likewise, do you really need so many interrupted sentences? Let people finish whenever you can. Within your text, a comma will often do the job of a dash or of ellipses and should be preferred. Never use more than one pair of dashes in a sentence.

✔ Restrict your use of the intrusive exclamation point almost exclusively to dialogue and feelings/thoughts. Otherwise, understatement is best. Not "The bull charged straight toward her!" but "The bull charged straight toward her."

✔ Avoid long, blocklike paragraphs. Break them up whenever possible.

✔ Don't overload a sentence with too much information. For example, don't describe how something looks *and* what it does in the same sentence. Not "The limousine, which was black with dark smoked windows, rounded the drive and stopped beneath the porte cochere," but "The limousine was black with dark smoked windows. It rounded the drive and stopped beneath the porte cochere."

✔ Watch your pronouns, which must agree with their antecedents. Never use *they* or *their* when you want to refer to either a male or a female. Though many people use this construction, it's wrong. Not "Every student knows they can come to me for help," but "Every student knows he or she can come to me for help." But this is cumbersome. Often it's easiest to rewrite the sentence in the plural: "Students know they can come to me for help."

THE FINER POINTS

Once you've completed your revisions and edits, type them into your manuscript on the computer or word processor. (If you use a typewriter, leave the edited manuscript for the moment.)

If your word-processing program has a spelling checker, run it. Do *not* run any sort of grammar checker; these are not intended for fiction.

Print out your manuscript again and read it through for typographical errors or misspellings the spelling checker didn't catch; for example, "They ate *there* breakfast."

When in doubt about a point of spelling, grammar or punctuation, refer to the following books, valuable additions to every novelist's library:

- *The Chicago Manual of Style* (Chicago: The University of Chicago Press, 14th ed., 1993)
- *Merriam-Webster's Collegiate Dictionary* (Springfield, MA: Merriam-Webster, Inc., 10th ed., 1993)
- *Words Into Type*, Skillin, Marjorie E., and Gay, Robert M. (Englewood Cliffs, NJ: Prentice-Hall, Inc., 3rd ed., 1986)

Also Helpful:

- Any good thesaurus
- *The Elements of Style*, Strunk, William, Jr., and White, E.B. (New York: Macmillan Publishing Co., 3rd ed., 1979)

Type corrections into your text on the computer, but don't print out your final manuscript just yet. In step fourteen you'll give your novel a few final touches.

To Recap
- Use The Novelist's Manual for Self-Editing to check story logic and strengthen your writing; edit directly on the hard copy of your manuscript.

- Enter editing changes on the computer or word processor (if you use a typewriter, leave the edited manuscript for the moment).
- Run the spelling checker, if you have one, but never a grammar checker.
- Print out the manuscript again and read for typos or misspellings the computer didn't catch.
- Invest in the best reference books you can afford.

Applying the Finishing Touches

In This Step
- Chapter division
- Adjusting manuscript length
- Title

You've no doubt noticed that your novel has no chapter breaks. The time to insert them is now, when everything else is to your satisfaction.

MAKING THE BREAK

Chapters are, structurally speaking, arbitrary divisions, more for the reader's convenience than anything else. How long should a chapter be? There's no right answer. Years ago chapters in novels were longer than they are now. Some writers and editors believed that with only a few chapter breaks, readers would be forced to keep reading. I don't believe that works anymore. Readers, their blocks of reading time shorter than ever, are going to put down your book whether there's a chapter break or not. You might as well make their lives easier by breaking your novel into smaller, more manageable pieces.

In fact, shorter chapters are more likely to pull a reader along: "Gee, I hate to stop now. How long is the next chapter? Only a few pages? Okay, *one* more. . . ." And so on to the end. An I'll-just-eat-one-more-peanut situation.

So short chapters are the order of the day. As for where to break, you have lots of freedom and only a few rules:

1. Divide chapters at space-break connectors.

2. End chapter one at the end of section #1.

3. End subsequent chapters at the end of *action* sections about your lead.

4. Aim for two to three sections per chapter, though this is not a hard-and-fast rule.

5. *Always* insert a chapter break after surprise #1, surprise #2 and surprise #3.

To insert your chapter breaks, simply end one chapter on one page and carry the start of the new chapter to the next page. The first page of a chapter should have thirteen lines of text. Type the chapter number centered two double-spaced lines above the text. Number your chapters consecutively throughout your novel.

ADJUSTMENTS

Now that your manuscript has chapters, you must see whether you hit the word length you were aiming for when you began— a word length, you'll recall, that's important to agents, editors, production managers, booksellers and readers.

Divide the target word length for your novel by 250. This is the number of pages your manuscript should contain.

You should be pretty close. But you'll have to do some tightening or expanding to hit the ideal number.

If you need additional pages, ask yourself:

• Can you add more chapter divisions? Each new chapter gains you half a page.

• Can you lengthen any of your action sections' conflict phases, heightening the drama?

• Should you lengthen the rational phase of any reaction section where perhaps you didn't show enough of the character's option-weighing process?

• Can you lengthen the emotional phase of any reaction section, intensifying the failure's impact on the character?

• Throughout the novel, have you remembered to show details of characters' everyday lives and occupations so sections do not play in a vacuum?

- Have you used space-break or run-together connectors where you might use summary connectors?
- If in dire need of more pages: You undoubtedly have characters referring to or thinking about action that has taken place offstage, between sections. Can you convert any of this action into actual, full-blown sections?

If you need fewer pages, ask yourself:

- Can you remove any chapter divisions? Each one removed reduces length by at least half a page.
- Can you tighten any of your action sections' conflict phases, being careful not to weaken the drama?
- Should you tighten the rational phase of any reaction section where perhaps you showed too much of the character's option-weighing process?
- Can you tighten the emotional phase of any reaction section without weakening the failure's impact on the character?
- Throughout the novel, can you cut extraneous details of characters' everyday lives and occupations?
- Have you used summary connectors where you might use space-break or run-together connectors?
- If in dire need of fewer pages: Can you convert any less dramatic sections into information that characters refer to or think about at the beginning of subsequent sections?

Try any or all of the above strategies to bring your manuscript to its target length.

A ROSE IS A ROSE

Your baby is beautiful but needs a name, a title. Perhaps you've had one all along; perhaps not.

From your reading in your target genre, you know if a certain kind of title is used for books like yours. If so, work within those parameters.

In general, your title should refer to what your novel is about. It should be striking. It should be original. It should be easy to pronounce and to remember (which usually means not too long).

If you're stumped, read through your manuscript for a phrase or an idea that might make for an interesting title.

Favorite sources of titles are Bartlett's *Familiar Quotations*, the Old and New Testaments, and the works of Shakespeare.

Titles can drive you crazy. Make a list of your favorites, mull them over for a few days and pick one. If your title is brilliant, it certainly won't hurt your chances of catching an editor's eye. If it's less than brilliant, it won't hurt a good book's chances of selling to an editor, who would likely help you find a new title.

Now that you have a title, you can make a title page. Type your name (not pseudonym), address and telephone number single-spaced in the upper left-hand corner of the page, against the top and left margins.

In the upper right-hand corner, against the top and right margins, type your manuscript's word count (the length you originally targeted); for example, 62,000 Words.

A third of the way down the page, center your title in all capital letters.

Double-space twice and center the words

A Novel by

Double-space twice and center your name or pseudonym.

The title page is not numbered. It will go on top of page 1.

Now type or print your manuscript on the 20-pound (74gsm) bond paper with 25 percent rag content, put your title page on top and place the pages loose in a manuscript or typing-paper box. That's how you'll submit it to agents and editors.

We'll talk about that in part 5.

To Recap

- Divide your novel into chapters, following the rules of chapter division on page 190.
- If necessary, adjust your manuscript to meet your original target word length.
- Give your novel a striking and appropriate title. Make a title page.
- Put your manuscript pages, with the title page on top, loose in a manuscript or typing-paper box.

Part 5

Marketing Your Novel

In This Part . . .

This part guides you in submitting your novel to agents and editors.

Producing a Knockout Proposal

In This Step
- The synopsis

Your novel is finished and ready to mail to an agent or editor. You shoot off a query letter (covered in step sixteen). The agent or editor asks to see your manuscript, *or* she asks to see a proposal: three chapters and a synopsis, or one chapter and a synopsis, or just a synopsis.

A *what*? A synopsis, a brief narrative summary of your novel. It's a vital marketing tool for a novelist, because it often has to do the entire job of enticing an agent or editor enough to want to read your novel. Think of the synopsis as a sales pitch for your book.

A synopsis has other uses, too. Later, when you sell your novel, your editor may ask you for a synopsis to be used as the basis for jacket or cover copy for your book. Other departments in the publishing house, such as Art or Sales or Publicity, may want to read your synopsis to get a quick idea of your story.

Even later, when it's time to sell your next novel, you'll be able to secure a contract solely on the basis of a synopsis and a few chapters, or just a synopsis. (The only time you should have to finish a book before selling it is the first time.) As you can see, the synopsis performs a number of important functions. It therefore deserves as careful attention as you've given the novel itself.

SYNOPSIS MECHANICS

The synopsis is formatted much like your manuscript. Use courier type; double-space all text; set your left, right and bottom

---

Deborah Price | Thriller
1317 Magnolia Lane | 120,000 Words
Shreveport, LA 71115 | Synopsis
(318) 555-6321

UNDER SUSPICION

SARA BRADFORD thought she and her husband, LANCE,
a Louisiana state senator, had a perfect marriage. Then she

---

margins at 1¼″ (3.2cm), your top margin at ½″ (1.3cm). Justify
the left margin only.

On every page except the first, type against the top and left
margins a slugline consisting of your last name, a slash, your
novel's title in capital letters, another slash and the word *Synopsis*,
like this: Price/UNDER SUSPICION/Synopsis. Number the
pages consecutively in the upper right-hand corner of the page,
against the top and right margins. The first line of text on each
page should be about ¾″ (1.9cm) below the slugline and page
number.

On the first page of your synopsis, against the top and left
margins, type single-spaced your name, address and telephone
number. Against the top and right margins, type single-spaced
your novel's genre, its word count and the word *Synopsis*. (The
first page of the synopsis is not numbered, though it is page 1.)

Double-space twice, center your novel's title in capital letters,
double-space twice again, and begin the text of your synopsis.

See above for how the synopsis of Sara Bradford's story would
begin.

SYNOPSIS BASICS

Before we get to the subtleties of writing the synopsis, here are
a few basic rules to be aware of.

1. The synopsis is always written in the present tense (called
the historical present tense).

2. The synopsis tells your novel's *entire* story. It doesn't leave out what's covered by the sample chapters submitted with it. Nor does it withhold the end of the story—for example, "who done it" in a murder mystery—in order to entice an agent or editor to want to see more. The synopsis is a miniature representation of your novel; to leave anything out is to defeat the purpose of the synopsis.

3. The synopsis should not run too long. An overlong synopsis also defeats its purpose. My rule is to aim for one page of synopsis for every twenty-five pages of manuscript. Thus a four-hundred-page manuscript calls for a sixteen-page synopsis. If you run a page or two over or under, don't worry about it.

4. To achieve this conciseness, write as clean and tight as you can. Cut extra adverbs and adjectives. Focus on your story's essential details. Let's say, for example, you have a section in which your lead meets another character for dinner at a chic French bistro to try to convince her to lend him some money. We don't need to know where they had dinner or what they ate or even exactly what was said. We need something on the order of "Ray meets Lenore for dinner and tries to convince her to lend him the money. Lenore refuses." Actual dialogue is rarely, if ever, needed in the synopsis.

5. Don't divide your synopsis by chapters; write one unified account of your story. You can use paragraphing to indicate a chapter or section break.

HOW TO MAKE YOUR SYNOPSIS SIZZLE

Now, keeping all of the above in mind, translate your manuscript into synopsis. Begin with your lead and her crisis as the hook of your synopsis. Then tell how your lead intends to solve the crisis (what is her story goal?). For example:

> BARBARA DANFORTH has never been especially fond of her brother-in-law, GRAHAM, but she would never have murdered him. Yet all the clues point to her as Graham's killer. She'll have to prove her innocence if she doesn't want to end up as dead as Graham.

PATRICK WARMAN, founder and director of Philadelphia's Friendship Street Shelter for runaway children, has always been careful to maintain a professional distance from the young people he helps. That's why he is especially horrified to realize he has fallen in love with PEARL, a teenage girl in his care. If he can't come to terms with these forbidden feelings, he'll lose everything he's worked for. Yet he can't bear to lose sixteen-year-old Pearl.

RITA RAYMOND is delighted when an employment agency sends her to work as a companion to a man recovering from an accident. She would never have accepted the job if she had known the man was her ex-husband, AARON. And damn if she isn't falling in love with him again. Yet Aaron was the cause of everything wrong in her life.

Soon after your problem hook, make sure you give us the vital details about your lead—age, occupation, marital status—(if you haven't already), as well as details of time (the present? the past?) and place.

Barbara, single at thirty-eight, has lived quietly in Rosemont, Texas, working as a stenographer and generally minding her own business. When her sister TRISH invited her to a party to celebrate the tenth anniversary of Trish's marriage to Graham, Barbara balked. She'd never liked Graham. But she accepted—her first mistake. Agreeing to let Graham take her for a moonlit walk around the couple's lavish estate was her second. . . .

Patrick, twenty-eight, has been married to MARIANNE for nine years, but although she helps at the shelter, their marriage is in name only. . . .

At twenty-nine, Rita has made peace with her life as a divorcée. She earns enough money as a high-school teacher to support herself and her seven-year-old daughter, ALLEGRA, though Allegra's severe asthma has been an emotional and financial strain. Even so, life these past five years without Aaron has been better than life was *with* him. . . .

Now continue telling your story, keeping to the main story points. Remember that the synopsis is not necessarily meant to convey the circumstances of *how* something happens; the happenings themselves are the concern here.

Most important, remember that *motivation and emotion are things that happen*; they are plot points, as important as any physical action a character might perform. Some of the worst synopses I've seen from would-be clients of my agency are dry and lifeless because these aspects have been left out.

Don't just tell us that Brandon tells Carla he's accepted the job in Sydney and that the next morning Carla has coffee at her friend Tanya's house and tells her the news. Tell us that when Brandon tells Carla he's accepted the job in Sydney, Carla sees her happy life collapsing around her, that she is devastated by this news. The next morning over coffee she pours her heart out to Tanya.

Don't just tell us that Jake Hammond stomps into the bank and dumps a sack of money on the president's desk, announcing he's repaying his loan. Tell us that Jake, full of angry self-righteousness at how the bank has treated his sister, stomps into the bank and dumps the money on the president's desk.

The agents and editors who will read and evaluate your synopsis are looking for the same things as your eventual readers: emotion and human drama. Bear down on these life-breathing aspects of your story and you can't go wrong.

Indicate other characters' story lines in your synopsis by beginning a new paragraph and describing the character's actions. Sometimes transitions such as "Meanwhile" or "Simultaneously" or "At the hotel" can help ground the reader in time and place.

As you write the synopsis, think of it as your novel in condensed form, and present events in the same order that they occur in the novel itself. Also, reveal information at the same points you do so in your novel.

Stay "invisible" in your synopsis; by this I mean several things. First, don't use devices that emphasize the mechanics of storytelling. One of these is the use of such headings as "Background," "Setting" and "Time" at the beginning of your synopsis. All of these elements should be smoothly woven into the narrative. Another such device is the use of character sketches or descriptions at the beginning or end of the synopsis. For one thing, they go into more detail than is appropriate for a synopsis. Second, they make it difficult for the agent or editor to follow your story: If he reads the synopsis first, it's meaningless because he has no information about the characters. If he reads the character sketches first, they are equally meaningless because the characters are not presented in the context of the story. Characters and story do not exist independently of each other. Give any important facts or background when you introduce a character.

In the text, type a character's name in capital letters the first time you use it—a technique borrowed from film treatments. Also, to avoid confusion, always refer to a character the same way throughout the synopsis (not "Dr. Martin" in one place, "the doctor" somewhere else and "Martin" somewhere else).

Another way to stay invisible is to avoid referring to the structural underpinnings of your story. When I was a kid, we used to go to an amusement park with a scary jungle ride which went through a dark tunnel where a native jumped out and scared us silly. One day as we floated through the tunnel and the native jumped out, I noticed that the figure of the native had come loose from its metal support. I could see ugly gray metal and a tangle of electrical wires. The ride was never the same after that.

That's how I feel when I can see the scaffolding of a synopsis—for example, "In a flashback, Myron. . . ." Better to simply say "Myron remembers. . . ." Don't write "At the darkest moment of her Point of Hopelessness . . ."; just tell what happens. Avoid "As the story begins . . ." or "As the story ends . . ."; just tell the story.

As you near the end of the synopsis and your story's resolution, quicken the pace by using shorter paragraphs and shorter sentences. A staccato effect increases the suspense.

Above all, never in your synopsis review your story, as "In a nerve-jangling confrontation . . ." or "In a heart-wrenching confession. . . ." This kind of self-praise is amateurish and inappropriate in a synopsis, which presents "just the (story) facts, ma'am"; let your story's attributes speak for themselves.

Once your synopsis is finished, polish, polish, polish! In many cases your synopsis will be your foot in the door, and many agents and editors will judge your storytelling and writing style from this selling piece alone. When I receive a synopsis containing misspellings, poor grammar and sloppy presentation, I do not ask to see the manuscript. I assume it will contain the same kinds of errors.

One final word of advice: Don't try to write your synopsis from your section sheets. It's not impossible, but you'll make your life more difficult than necessary. The section sheets contain too great a level of detail; if you translate them, you're likely to find your synopsis running too long. Work from your manuscript, reading each section or chapter and then retelling it briefly, as you might if you were telling your story to a friend.

Writing the synopsis is an art you should become proficient in. A masterful synopsis starts selling your novel to an agent or editor before she even looks at your manuscript. In fact, a few times during my career I have read a synopsis so well-crafted that later I felt I had read the book! That's real magic.

A sample synopsis appears in the Appendix.

To Recap
- A well-written synopsis is a vital marketing tool for your novel, both before and after it's sold.
- Follow correct manuscript format.
- Write the synopsis in the present tense.
- Tell the entire story, with events in the same order as in the novel.
- Aim for a length of one synopsis page for every twenty-five manuscript pages.
- Focus on story essentials.
- Start with a problem-and-story-goal hook.
- Include characters' motivations and emotions.
- Don't let story mechanics show.

Approaching Agents and Editors

In This Step
- The role of the agent
- Getting an agent
- Submitting to editors
- Rejection

Your manuscript and synopsis are all dressed up; now where do they go? To literary agents or editors or perhaps both, depending on the kind of novel you've written.

Let's talk about agents first. Do you need one? Not necessarily, though an agent—a *good* agent—can have a big impact on your career. A bad agent can have a big impact, too, but it's not the kind of impact you're looking for.

WHAT AN AGENT CAN DO FOR YOU

An agent is a writer's guide to the book-publishing industry, keeping track of its ever-changing rules and players in order to get the writer's work in front of the right editors at the right publishing houses at the right times. Knowing the parameters of the market for a given genre of novel, the agent can negotiate the best possible deal for the writer. Then the agent makes it his business to see that all goes smoothly and appropriately as the book moves through the publishing process, from first manuscript to first publication and beyond.

An agent has contacts a writer usually doesn't, enabling the agent to sell subsidiary rights including magazine serialization,

British publication, foreign-language translation, and film and TV rights.

A good agent can do even more. She can be a writer's trusted business and creative partner, often the one constant in an industry where editors change and exchange jobs with alarming frequency.

The role of agents has expanded to the point that many act as concept editors themselves, helping writers conceive and develop story ideas and then connecting the finished products with the right editors. In short, an agent is a catalyst, matching editors' needs with those of her writers. An agent can even become a writer's friend; often it's an inevitable development, given the close nature of the relationship.

Perhaps most importantly, with an agent taking care of business, you have more time to do what a writer should do: *write*.

WHAT AGENTS DON'T DO

Movies, television and even books have presented a distorted and highly romanticized view of the agent's role. An agent does not (and should not be expected to):

- Sell work that's unsalable
- Teach people how to write (unless he publishes a book like this one, but that's different)
- Act as an editor (beyond making general suggestions)
- Serve as a publicist or public relations agent
- Play the role of secretary, travel agent or Broadway-tickets procurer
- Act as a lawyer (though some agents are also lawyers)
- Solve a writer's personal problems
- Lend money
- Be available outside of regular business hours, except by appointment

DO YOU NEED AN AGENT?

You may need an agent, if only out of pure practicality. Many publishers will no longer consider unagented material. You can bet that at these houses, the "slush pile" is a thing of the past, despite all those wonderful old stories about million-copy *New York Times* best-sellers that arrived over the transom. Few publishers believe it is cost effective to have editors or even editorial assistants spending precious hours slogging through thousands of rejects in search of that one publishable manuscript. And why should they, when the savvy agents are screening material for them *and* doing it at no cost to them. You may need an agent just to get your novel onto an editor's desk.

Because an agent knows from experience what financial and other contractual terms are reasonable for a given property, he will almost always get a writer a better deal than the writer would have gotten if she had negotiated the deal herself. Editors are businesspeople, employed by their publishing houses, charged with acquiring the highest quality books at the most favorable terms for the houses. Why should they pay more than they have to? This means that if an editor is buying your novel from you directly, and you're not aware that the offer could be a lot better, the editor is not going to volunteer that information. When does the editor have to pay more? When an agent is involved.

Believe it or not, when it comes to business matters, most editors prefer to deal with agents rather than directly with writers. Agents and editors speak the same language. Agents know which contract terms are negotiable and whether terms are reasonable, and are less likely to waste editors' time. Negotiations progress far more quickly and smoothly; the agent explains terms and procedures to the writer along the way.

Having an agent also allows you to play "good cop, bad cop," enabling you to keep your relationship with your editor unadversarial and unsullied by vulgar monetary matters. If conflicts do arise between you and your editor—and they probably will somewhere along the way—your agent can step in and smooth them out. Few creative professionals are able to swap hats from artist to businessperson without one role affecting the other.

CAN A NEWCOMER GET AN AGENT?

If you've heard that nonsense about there being a catch-22 for unpublished writers—you can't get an agent unless you've been published, but you can't get published unless you have an agent—forget about it. It's untrue. If your work has merit, you *can* get an agent, even if you've never published a word. It just may take some persistence.

While agents are less likely to take on unpublished writers (since published writers are more apt to keep getting published, generating the commissions on which we agents live), most will take on a writer whose work excites them and they feel they can sell. For example, last year I took on three wonderfully talented, unpublished novelists; all three now have multibook contracts with major publishers.

TARGETING AGENTS

Before you approach agents, you must decide which ones you think would be right for you. Agents have different specialties, different personalities, different tastes. When you approach one, you should believe she's right for you and your work.

I once phoned a writer to offer representation on a manuscript she had submitted to me. Her response: "But I . . . I don't know anything about you!" Then why on earth, I asked, had she submitted her work to me? "I don't know. I just pulled your name out of some directory."

Don't do that.

How do you find out which agents handle what—specifically, which agents handle *what you wrote*? Research. Selecting an agent may be one of the most important decisions of your career, so the research will be more than worth your time.

Personal Contacts

Do you have a novelist friend, colleague or relative who has an agent who handles what she writes? Ask this writer whether she might put in a good word for you, or at the very least, whether you might use her name when you approach the agent. Many agents find new writers through this sort of referral.

Do you know any writing teachers? Booksellers? Book reviewers? Publisher's sales reps or publicists? Librarians? Are you a member of a writing club or organization or a critique group? Any of these people may know agents—or other people who know agents. There really are only six degrees of separation. Again, ask for a good word or permission to mention the person's name.

Association of Authors' Representatives

The Association of Authors' Representatives (AAR), of which I am a member, is an organization of literary and dramatic agents. (It was founded in 1991 through the merger of the Society of Authors' Representatives and the Independent Literary Agents Association.) This self-policing group requires its members to meet certain professional standards specified in the organization's bylaws and to agree to subscribe to its Canon of Ethics. For example, the AAR prohibits its members from charging clients or potential clients for reading and evaluating material, a practice it believes "is subject to serious abuse that reflects badly on our profession."

Members of the AAR keep informed on current publishing issues through meetings, seminars and panel discussions. Committees work to better the status of writers; for example, one such committee worked with publishers to improve the format of royalty statements.

Though the AAR will not recommend specific members, it will send you a listing of its members, along with its Canon of Ethics, a list of suggested questions to ask agents who offer you representation, and a brochure about the organization. Send your request with a check or money order for $7 and a self-addressed business-size envelope affixed with adequate postage to: Member List, Association of Authors' Representatives, 10 Astor Place, 3rd Floor, New York, NY 10003.

The AAR listing is a good start because its members place such high value on honesty and professionalism. (Bear in mind, however, that some highly reputable agencies do not belong to the AAR.) But this listing indicates only whether members are literary or dramatic agents, whether they handle adult or children's material, and if they are accepting material (you can rule out those who aren't). You'll have to research further to refine your list.

Publications

A number of publications can help you get the facts on agents you're considering.

Literary Market Place. Known in the publishing industry as the *LMP*, this annual directory of the book-publishing industry is available in most larger libraries' reference sections. It contains a listing of active literary agents, including key personnel, specialties and policies.

Market Guides. The annual *Guide to Literary Agents*, published by Writer's Digest Books, provides detailed listings of agents' specialties and recent sales. Writer's Digest Books also publishes its Marketplace series of genre-specific guides. These include *Mystery Writer's Sourcebook* and *Science Fiction and Fantasy Writer's Sourcebook*, which contain lists of agents active in these genres.

Magazines. Keep an eye on trade magazines (also available at larger libraries)—most notably *Publishers Weekly*, which runs several regular columns that report on recent agent deals of note.

Watch any fanzines (magazines put together by fans) in your target genre for names of agents active in your field. Also useful are the many publications that report news and trends in the genres—for example, *Locus* in science fiction, *Mystery Scene* in mystery and *Romantic Times* in romance. Visit a large newsstand to see what's available.

Books. As you continue to read books in your target genre, comb acknowledgments for agents' names.

Compile a list of authors in your genre whose work you admire and/or whose readers you think would also enjoy your work. At your library, look up these writers in the following directories to find the names of the writers' agents: *Contemporary Authors*; *Directory of American Poets and Fiction Writers*; *International Authors and Writers Who's Who*; *Who's Who in Writers, Editors, and Poets*; and *Writers Directory*. For children's and young adults' writers, consult *Something About the Author*.

Seminars, Workshops, Conferences and Conventions. You're always likely to find agents at the many gatherings for writers and their fans held around the country throughout the year. You can also be pretty sure these agents are looking for new clients: That's one of the reasons they're there.

Take advantage (courteously, of course) of any opportunity to meet these agents personally; conferences often arrange brief one-on-one meetings between agents and attendees. At this meeting, tell the agent your novel's genre and the hook from your synopsis. Don't try to give the agent material at this meeting, however; it's generally considered bad form. Do give her your business card, perhaps jotting the title of your novel and its genre on the back. Then query the agent by mail shortly after the conference is over, referring to your meeting. (More on querying shortly.)

At these conferences you'll also meet editors, and often they are willing to recommend agents. Most editors, in order to not appear to play favorites, will furnish the names of several agents they respect and enjoy doing business with.

WHICH AGENT IS RIGHT FOR YOU?

From your research, you've compiled a list of agents who look like good possibilities for representing you and your work. They are active in your genre, are accepting new clients and are reputed to be ethical and professional in their dealings with publishers and writers.

If you have met any of the agents, try to imagine what it would be like to work with each one. Is this someone with whom you would feel comfortable discussing your work and writing-career goals? Someone from whom you wouldn't resent receiving disappointing news or criticism about your work? Are you intimidated by this person? Somehow uneasy? There are as many different styles of agents as there are agents, and only you know which style is right for you. Follow your gut instinct: If this is someone you feel comfortable talking to, someone you can see yourself working with over the long haul, give that person a try.

If you suspect an agent might be right for you but have not met him or her, perhaps you can find someone who knows the agent and ask some questions. If you're thinking of approaching an agent to whom you've been referred, ask the person who referred you what the agent is like to work with, what his or her working style is. Warm and nurturing? Brisk and businesslike? Somewhere in between? At seminars, workshops, conferences and conventions you can ask editors if they have worked with the agent you have in mind, and if so, how they would describe the agent's overall professional manner.

If there's absolutely no way for you to get an idea of an agent's style but you still feel he could be right for you, approach the agent anyway. The worst that could happen is that in talking with the agent, later you decide it's not a good match. At this point you politely say that you don't think you would be best suited to the agent's talents and thank him for his time.

READING FEES

Before we get into submission procedures, let's talk about reading fees, which you may encounter. You already know that the Association of Authors' Representatives frowns on this practice and prohibits its members from engaging in it.

As long as there have been agents, there have also been people who call themselves agents (and anyone can call himself a literary agent) but who do not really make a living selling books to publishers. Instead, they take advantage of naive, hopeful beginners who are only too glad to pay to have their material considered, and often to have their manuscripts "professionally edited" by these same "agents."

On the other hand, some reputable, legitimate agents charge modest reading fees; they maintain that it's the only way they can afford to consider the work of prospective clients.

Much controversy still surrounds the ethics of charging reading fees. The important question, however, is: Is the agent reputable and honest? Is she really an *agent*? If your research tells you yes to both questions, and the agent to whom you would like to submit your novel charges a reading fee, write the agent a letter inquiring about the fee policy. Ultimately, you should have the answers to the following four questions:

1. Is this a onetime fee, or will you have to pay it again on subsequent submissions?

2. Will you have to pay the fee again if you submit a revised manuscript?

3. Will the fee be refunded or applied to future commissions if the agent takes you on?

4. What, exactly, will you get for your money? Just a reading, followed by a yes or no, or some criticism and analysis?

There are no right answers to these questions; just be sure you know what you're getting into so that there will be no surprises later.

THE QUERY LETTER

Some agents will state in their listings in directories or market guides that they wish to receive more than just a query letter from prospective clients; for example, they may want a query with a synopsis and three chapters. If an agent you wish to approach includes such information in his listing, by all means comply. Otherwise, fall back on the time-honored convention of never sending material to an agent "cold"—without prior contact and, of course, the agent's invitation to do so. Material sent without this contact and invitation is an *unsolicited submission*. It's unprofessional to throw a six-pound Jiffy Bag at someone who's never even heard of you. The agent probably won't read it and may not even bother to return it to you, even if you've enclosed a stamped, self-addressed envelope.

A query letter is always the most effective way to approach an agent, even one you've already met. Like any business letter, the query should be professional and concise, ideally no more than one single-spaced page.

In your letter, state your novel's genre, title and word length; then tell briefly what it's about. Perhaps you'll want to say you believe your novel will appeal to readers of a certain author's books.

Provide any relevant information about yourself: previous publishing credits (for example, short stories or articles), writers' organizations to which you belong, awards or citations you've received for your writing, and any pertinent background (for instance, you've written a crime novel based on your experiences as a criminal lawyer).

Address your letter to the agent by name, not to "Dear Sir or Madam" or "Gentlemen" or "Dear Agent" or "To whom it may concern" (I've seen all of these and more). And—need I say it?—no photocopied form letters with the agent's name and address typed in; how seriously would *you* consider a letter like that?

Don't include anything with your query letter (no one-page synopsis, photo of yourself, newspaper clipping proving the timeliness of your novel—nothing) except a stamped, self-addressed business-size envelope, folded in thirds, for the agent's reply.

The sample query letter in Figure 13 demonstrates these guidelines.

The agent's reply may be a no, in which case you cross that name off your agent list and try the next one; or the reply could be a request for a synopsis, a synopsis and the first chapter, a synopsis and the first three chapters, or your complete manuscript.

Whatever the request, you're ready. Your material is, of course, just waiting for this moment—always strike while the agent is hot. Prepare a brief cover letter, thanking the agent for her willingness to read your material, which you are enclosing. Include a self-addressed envelope large and strong enough, and stamped with enough postage, for the return of your material. I don't believe in telling the agent it's unnecessary to return the material because I think it sends a negative subliminal message to the agent about the material's value before he even reads it.

If you're sending a synopsis or a synopsis and chapters, place the pages loose in a manila folder. Then put the cover letter, folder and return envelope in a 9″ × 12″ (22.9cm × 30.5cm) envelope and mail it.

Do the agent a favor and use mailers padded with plastic instead of pulped newspaper. When the latter type burst—and more often than not, they do—the agent is treated to an unwanted indoor blizzard. Your manuscript doesn't look too great with bits of newsprint clinging to it, either.

DEBORAH PRICE
1317 Magnolia Lane
Shreveport, LA 71115
(318) 555-6321

September 15, 1998

Mr. Evan Marshall
The Evan Marshall Agency
Six Tristam Place
Pine Brook, New Jersey 07058-9445

Dear Mr. Marshall:

I have just completed a 120,000-word thriller entitled *Under Suspicion*. It's the story of Sara Bradford, a police chief in a small Louisiana town, who is married to a state senator. Sara's happy marriage is overshadowed by distrust when she learns that her husband may be living a dark secret life—as a member of the Ku Klux Klan. Sara must learn the truth before it's too late.

I think my novel will appeal to fans of John Grisham and Steve Martini, who have had a strong influence on my work.

I am a native of Louisiana and, until my retirement, practiced law as a partner in a small firm in New Orleans. I have based much of my novel on my experiences.

Over the past year, *Southern Suspense Journal* has published two of my short stories.

May I send you *Under Suspicion*?

I look forward to hearing from you.

Sincerely,

Deborah Price

Deborah Price

Enclosure: SASE

Figure 13: A Sample Query Letter

If you're sending your manuscript, place your cover letter in the box with your loose manuscript pages; then put the box and return mailer in a padded mailing bag, staple it a few times and mail it.

How to mail it? Priority Mail is fine. Don't use any method that requires a signature at the other end—an annoying inconvenience if the agent is not in the office when delivery is attempted.

Don't insure your package or ask for a return receipt, which also requires a signature. (If you want a receipt to prove you sent your material, in case of possible theft or plagiarism, then you don't know enough about this agent to know he wouldn't do something like that, and you shouldn't be submitting to him in the first place.) Try to make things as easy as possible for the agent.

Make sure you have a copy of whatever you're sending out— a hard copy in addition to what's on your hard drive or diskette. Keep a record of your submissions—a copy of the submission letter will do—and mark your wall calendar with the date the material was sent out.

Don't call the agent's office "just to make sure the package arrived safely." Unless the postal service returns it to you, figure it did.

Can you submit to more than one agent simultaneously? Certainly, but professional courtesy requires that you inform an agent if he is not considering your work exclusively. Some agents will only consider material exclusively; they'll usually say so when they ask to see your work. Usually these agents will offer to give you an answer within a few weeks in exchange for this special consideration.

SIGNING ON

Hooray! An agent offers to represent you, and it's the beginning of a beautiful relationship. If, that is, no unpleasant surprises arise in the course of your working together. To prevent such surprises, you and your agent should be clear on the details of this relationship from the start.

What are the agent's working procedures, and how can you make sure they mesh with yours? For example, if your agent resents clients calling monthly for a status report and you intend to check in every Friday afternoon, you've both got a problem. Agree on what's reasonable in terms of keeping in touch—probably something in between the two extremes above—but rest assured that if your agent has good news, she'll call. If you would like copies of rejection letters from editors, tell your agent; on the other hand, let her know if the only feedback you want is "I'll buy it!" There's no right or wrong way here, just what works for you and your agent.

Learn how the agent works in terms of foreign rights: Does he work with coagents overseas or through a foreign-rights agency in New York? Does he work with a coagent in Hollywood for film and TV rights?

What are the agent's commissions on various kinds of sales? Many agents charge a 15 percent commission on domestic sales (some agencies still charge 10 percent) and 20 percent on the sale of British and translation rights, and film and TV rights. Make sure you understand all these details from the start.

For specific points to explore with an agent before you agree to work together, I would again recommend that you obtain the AAR's list of suggested questions.

Though at one time agents worked with writers on the basis of nothing more than a handshake, many nowadays use some form of written representation agreement. This agreement will set out commissions and other charges your agent may deduct from your earnings for extraordinary expenses. These may include: long-distance telephone calls, postage, photocopying, legal fees, messengers, shipping and the cost of books and advance reading copies for use in selling subsidiary rights.

The agreement may also stipulate a term of representation—a year, two years, even five. Though you'll no doubt go into this relationship with every wish to make it last indefinitely, you never know what the future holds, so the shorter the term—if one is required—the better. Best, of course, is a stipulation that either party may terminate the relationship at any time by means of a letter, usually with notice of a month to several months so the agent can finish any deals he has initiated.

SUBMITTING DIRECTLY TO EDITORS

A few publishing houses will still consider unagented material. You can find out which ones they are by checking the publisher listings in the *LMP*. Also, publishers that issue tip sheets will usually consider material directly from writers and will say so on the tip sheet.

You'll still need to query, though: These publishers will accept *unagented* submissions, not unsolicited ones. Follow the same procedure as you would for an agent, being sure to write to a specific editor *by name*. If you want to submit to a particular publisher but do not have an editor's name, call the editorial department and ask who the appropriate editor would be for your submission.

IF AN EDITOR BITES

Suppose an editor wants to buy your novel. It's still not too late to get an agent to take over the contractual negotiations, if you so desire. This is, in fact, a quite common occurrence. As soon as you know that the editor intends to make an offer on your book, tell her you want to have an agent represent you, then politely request that the editor wait and discuss the terms with the agent, who will be in touch shortly. The editor may grumble a little, but if she shows a real reluctance to deal with an agent, she was probably hoping to take advantage of your naïveté.

A word of warning: Any terms you agree to (as in, "That sounds fine," in response to an editor's offer of a $500 advance), you'll be stuck with, since an agent cannot ethically come in and change terms that have already been negotiated. So keep your lips buttoned.

Here's where you approach one of your agents of choice; and a phone call *is* OK in this case since time is of the essence. Simply tell the agent an editor wants to buy your book and you are looking for an agent to handle this and future deals.

Just because an editor wants to buy your book, however, don't expect your agent of choice to whisk you off to the Grill Room at The Four Seasons for lunch. Most agents will still want a quick look at what you're selling and perhaps at anything else you have in the works. Though the agent may be assured of a commission on this project, he will want to decide whether he can do something for you in the long run.

Another word of warning: You might think, "I'll just negotiate this deal myself, save the agent's commission and, once I've sold a book, pick up an agent for my next deal." That's possible, but the money you save may be far outweighed by what you could lose by locking yourself into unfavorable contractual terms (for example, a next-book option that requires you to submit a complete manuscript)—terms an agent, if pulled into the picture too late, may be powerless to remedy.

If you can't get an agent to handle your deal, or you simply want to do it yourself, get any of several books that cover book-contract basics and read fast. An excellent source is *The Writer's Legal Guide*, by Tad Crawford and Tony Lyons (Writer's Digest Books).

THE R WORD

Inevitably, as you begin to submit your material and even further along in your writing career, you will encounter the R word: *rejection*. This powerful word can have a strong negative effect on writers who don't think about it the right way.

First, rejection is inevitable. Getting an agent or hooking an editor relies to such a large part on what is on these people's plates at a given moment that it's impossible not to encounter people who can't use what you've got right now. Agents' client lists wax and wane; an agent with more than she can handle may have to turn down a novel even if she likes it. A publisher with enough inventory (books purchased and waiting to be published) for two years may have to turn down a novel even if it's highly publishable. So in order to find people with the right open slots at the right time, you *must* get past the others and keep looking.

Second, a rejection isn't an absolute condemnation of your novel; it's *one person's judgment*, and that judgment is purely subjective. Have you ever played that game where you open a fortune cookie, read your fortune and add the words *in bed*? "You will meet a dark stranger—in bed!" You get the idea. When I receive a letter from an editor turning down a novel by one of my clients, I add the words *in your opinion*. "The writing is a bit flat—in your opinion!"

That's all it is—one person's opinion about a piece of art. And when it comes to art, there are no absolutes.

I'm not saying I'm not open to honest, helpful criticism. I am, and I encourage my clients to be, too. But I have to see the same criticism several times before I'll entertain it as valid. Don't get me wrong; I respect editors and their opinions. It's just that every editor seems to have a different one.

If an agent or an editor comments negatively on your novel, smile graciously, be thankful for the time the person spent on your material, and figure he just didn't get it. Most important, know that your material is still as good as it was before the negative comment.

Third, rejection isn't personal. *Rejection* is such a charged word. It conjures images of editors whacking manuscripts off their desks with a great "Yuck!"—or whacking *you* off their desks. That's not at all what they're doing. They're simply saying, "I'll pass." In almost all cases, of course, they don't even know you. Yet many writers crumple at this judgment of their "babies," taking it as a personal affront. Some vow never to write again, and they're barely out of the gate!

Think about us agents: We get rejected all the time when clients' material comes back. If we let rejection stop us, we'd be out of business fast. More often than not those good books eventually find their rightful homes. Sometimes it takes a lot of tries (my record is forty-three).

You have to keep trying, because when all is said and done, it's all quite haphazard. You may hit your agent or editor on try number one or try number sixteen. Wouldn't it be a shame if you never made try number sixteen because some agent's or editor's opinion got you depressed and you stopped submitting, or worse yet, stopped writing?

Don't stop. Your head and your heart are full of wonderful stories—stories the world deserves to read.

THE JOURNEY BEGINS

With this plan, you now have at your disposal the means of finishing not just one novel but many. The Marshall Plan is not the only way to write a novel, but this way works every time. Even if, as you advance in your writing career, you try new methods and techniques, maybe judiciously break a few rules, this system will always be here to fall back on as a proven way to get those books finished.

Finishing—that's half the recipe for success. Geniuses who never finish never get published. Maybe you're a genius, maybe not—it doesn't matter. The world places far more value on someone who produces than on someone who just talks or thinks about producing. We can't read and enjoy novels that never leave that bottom desk drawer.

The epigraph at the beginning of this book is a quote from Jane Ellice Hopkins with which I fervently agree: "Genius only means an infinite capacity for taking pains." To you as a writer that means working to make your novels the best they can be.

Novel writing *is* hard work. But it's hard work you'd better learn to enjoy if you want to make it as a novelist. The other half of the recipe for success is *staying power*; the successful novelists are in it for the long haul.

Most of them see their careers as a journey—of learning, growing, aiming higher and growing some more. They're in this business of telling stories because they love it and couldn't *not* do it, not because they want to make a lot of money (though some have found themselves rich).

Don't do it for the money. You can find easier ways to make money. Do it because you love it. Give yourself time to grow, to take pains. Believe in yourself but be humble enough to keep learning. Savor not just the dream of success but also the journey to reach that dream.

One day, perhaps when you least expect it, that dream will come true.

To Recap

- An agent is a writer's guide and advisor, a link to the publishing world.

- Agents *will* take on talented unpublished writers.
- Research possible agents through personal contacts; the Association of Authors' Representatives; publications; and seminars, workshops, conferences and conventions.
- Try to get an idea of the working style of an agent you're interested in approaching.
- If you approach an agent who charges a reading fee, know exactly what you'll get for your money and if you'll have to pay more fees in the future should the agent take you on.
- Query agents before sending material, unless they have specified otherwise.
- In your query letter, include your novel's genre, title and word count; a brief description of the novel; relevant information about yourself.
- If an agent offers representation, ask the right questions about how she works.
- Some publishers still accept submissions from writers; query them first.
- If an editor wants to make an offer on your novel, you can bring in an agent to negotiate the deal.
- If you handle your own deal, consult a guide to book-contract negotiations first.
- Ignore rejection and keep writing.
- Keep producing, keep learning and enjoy the journey to success.

Glossary

This glossary defines important terms used in the Marshall Plan. To see where a term is used in the book, refer to the index. Words set in italics are defined in the glossary.

Action mode. A manner of fiction writing in which every action is dramatized chronologically with no summary.

Action section. A *section* in which a character pursues a *section goal* he believes will help him achieve the *story goal*.

Background mode. A manner of fiction writing in which background information is presented.

Beginning. The first quarter of the novel, in which the *lead* experiences the *crisis* and sets her *story goal*, all characters are introduced and all background information is presented.

Character fact list. A compilation of basic facts about a character, necessary to establish before plotting the novel.

Confidant. A character who serves as an advisor to and sounding board for the *lead*.

Connector. A device for connecting one section with the next. The three types of connectors are the *space-break connector*, *run-together connector* and *summary connector*.

Crisis. A disastrous event that forces the *lead* to set a *story goal* of restoring his life to normal.

Crisis criteria. Conditions a *crisis* must satisfy to work effectively in a novel. There are three crisis criteria: (1) The crisis must be *genre* appropriate, (2) it must turn the *lead*'s life upside down in a negative way, and (3) it must capture the writer's imagination.

Dialogue mode. A manner of fiction writing in which dialogue is of central importance.

End. The last quarter of the novel, in which all *story line*s are resolved—the *lead* finally vanquishing the *opposition* and achieving the *story goal*.

External conflict. A situation or circumstance that stands in the way of two characters' entering into a romantic relationship.

Feelings/thoughts mode. A manner of fiction writing in which a character's feelings and thoughts are presented.

Flashback. Past story action presented as its own full-fledged *action section*.

Genre. A category of fiction, such as horror, romance or mystery. Your target genre is the type of novel in which you have decided to specialize.

Internal conflict. An emotional resistance within a character which makes him or her reluctant to commit to a romantic relationship.

Lead. A novel's main character—its hero or heroine. A novel is first and foremost about the lead's pursuit of her *story goal*.

Lead's subplot. A *story line*, secondary to the main *story line*, in which the *lead* pursues a separate goal.

Line. A publisher's program of novels of a particular genre; for example, a line of romances or Westerns.

Main story line. The *lead*'s pursuit of the *story goal*.

Middle. The central portion of the novel, constituting half its length. In the middle, the principal action of the lead's pursuit of the *story goal* takes place.

Opposition. The character who most stands in the way of the *lead*'s achieving her *story goal*.

Point of Hopelessness. The *lead*'s darkest moment, directly following the *Worst Failure*, when it appears he has failed to achieve the *story goal* and all hope is lost.

Reaction section. A *section* in which a character responds to what happened in his previous *action section*.

Romantic involvement. A character who is the object of the *lead*'s romantic and/or sexual interest.

Run-together connector. A *section*-joining device consisting of running one *section* right from the last, with no break in the text other than the start of a new paragraph.

Saving Act. A heroic action the *lead* takes to defeat the *opposition* and achieve the *story goal*.

Section. A single unit of story action in the novel. A section can be an *action section* or a *reaction section*.

Section character. The focal character of a *section*, from whose viewpoint the *section* is planned and written.

Section goal. The short-term goal (toward the *story goal*) a character pursues within a single *action section*.

Section sheet. A template on which you plan what will happen in a *section*.

Space-break connector. A *section*-joining device consisting of a blank line or space between *sections*.

Story goal. The objective a character pursues throughout the novel to solve the *crisis*.

Story goal criteria. Conditions a *lead*'s *story goal* must satisfy. There are four story goal criteria: (1) The *lead* must seek possession of or relief from something, (2) he must face terrible consequences if he fails to achieve the *story goal*, (3) he must have a worthy motivation for pursuing the *story goal*, and (4) he must face tremendous odds in pursuing the *story goal*.

Story idea. The *lead*'s *Suppose* (*crisis*) combined with his *story goal*.

Story line. A distinct plot thread in which a character pursues a goal.

Subplot. See *story line*.

Summary connector. A *section*-joining device consisting of a paragraph or two of summarized action.

Summary mode. A manner of fiction writing in which story action is presented in a condensed, narrative form.

Suppose. An idea for a *crisis* for a novel's *lead*.

Surprise. A shocking development in the *lead*'s main *story line*. A novel has three surprises: (1) at the end of the *beginning*, (2) at the novel's midpoint, and (3) at the end of the middle.

Synopsis. A brief narrative summary of a novel.

Tip sheet. A set of guidelines, issued by a publisher, to writing for a specific *line* of books.

Viewpoint character. The character through whose awareness and perceptions a *section* is planned and written.

Viewpoint writing. A method of writing fiction in which everything is filtered through the perceptions and awareness of a specific *viewpoint character*.

Word length. The customary length of a given type of novel, expressed in the number of words.

Worst Failure. The ultimate confrontation between the *lead* and the *opposition*, in which the *lead* utterly fails (see *Point of Hopelessness*).

Wrap-Up. The novel's final *section*, following the *lead*'s attainment of the *story goal*, in which we see her in her restored state of happiness.

Appendix

A SAMPLE SYNOPSIS

The following synopsis is by Daniel Steven, a client of my agency who writes superb novels of suspense. His first, *Final Remedy*, was published by HarperCollins Publishers. HarperCollins bought Dan's second novel, *Clinical Trials*, on the basis of this synopsis. The book has since been published to high acclaim.

Note first that this synopsis at approximately eighteen pages is the ideal length for the novel it represents: At one page of synopsis per twenty-five manuscript pages, it's right on the mark at a total of 450 manuscript pages, or 112,500 words.

Dan deviates slightly from the practice of beginning the synopsis with the lead's crisis-and-story-goal hook and starts instead with the quick vignette of Jason Conner delivering his explosive letter to the White House. (These quick other-character vignettes can be effective as long as the lead is brought in quickly, as Dan has done here.) We then switch to Nicole Girard (the romantic involvement) jumping from her hospital window. The novel's lead, Dylan Ice, is brought into the story in the context of Nicole's jump, which in fact constitutes the beginning of his crisis.

Dan smoothly integrates pertinent background information as he introduces each character; for example: "Fletcher, fifty-eight, is a wealthy televangelist in the Pat Robertson mold." We know enough to understand this character in the context of the story.

The synopsis delivers only the main points of the story without unnecessary details: "Dylan commits her to a drug rehabilitation program." That's all we need to know here.

Note the use of transitional devices to ground us in time and place: "The next day," "At the same time," "Back in Washington," "At about the same time," "The following morning," "Back home."

Observe the motivation and emotional details which give the synopsis strength and color: ". . . for personal reasons, he doesn't like the idea of involuntary commitment"; "He is upset . . .";

"Dylan feels compelled . . ."; "But now he's more determined than ever . . ."; "Dylan is in shock"; "Dylan is tired of being reactive."

Finally, note how in his Wrap-up Dan ends on the note of a possible romantic commitment between Dylan and his romantic involvement, Nicole.

Daniel Steven	Political Thriller
% The Evan Marshall Agency	112,500 Words
Six Tristam Place	Synopsis
Pine Brook, New Jersey 07058-9445	

CLINICAL TRIALS

In Washington, D.C., JASON CONNER, thirty-five, a thin blond man, jumps over the fence in front of the White House and walks purposefully toward the mansion. It's broad daylight, and Secret Service agents are ready for him. When Conner reaches into his coat to remove an envelope, a young cop panics and shoots Conner through the heart. CRAIG OLSON, the president's closest advisor, is the only one who reads the contents of the envelope, and he reacts to it as if he's stepped on a snake.

Several years later, in a Midwest hospital, NICOLE GIRARD, thirty-eight, yanks an intravenous line out of her arm, gets out of bed, and climbs onto a second-floor window ledge. In the open courtyard below is a ceremony dedicating the hospital's new AIDS research center.

Nicole watches as the center's director, DR. MARK ARGENT, forty-two, steps to the podium and introduces the center's primary financial contributor, the REV. VERNON FLETCHER. Fletcher, fifty-eight, is a wealthy televangelist in the Pat Robertson mold. Among the spectators is DYLAN ICE. Dylan, twenty-seven, is the product of an interracial marriage between two hippies in the mid-1960s. His childhood was spent in communes and group homes, and being biracial didn't make life any easier. Perhaps as an antidote to the turmoil, he has become a rather conservative, upwardly mobile lawyer. He works in the law firm representing the Rev. Fletcher's fundamentalist organization, and is also the guardian of his younger sister, a sixteen-year-old hellion named JANIS (after Janis Joplin).

The Rev. Fletcher is partly through his speech when Nicole jumps off the window ledge, landing in the grassy area behind the presentation platform. Climbing onto the platform, Nicole screams at Dr. Argent, "Vampire! Bloodsucker!" Argent tries to pull her away, but she attacks him with teeth and nails, then runs to the end of the platform and jumps off, falling onto the brick courtyard. She is knocked unconscious.

After Nicole is taken to the Emergency Room and the dedication ceremony concludes, Dr. Argent and his wife, LINDA ARGENT (a registered nurse and Argent's assistant), meet with one of the dignitaries on the platform: PETER ROSATI, director of the National Institute of Allergy and Infectious Diseases (NIAID) at the National Institutes of Health in Washington (NIH). They discuss Nicole's case, and it's clear there's something special about her.

The next day Dylan Ice is called into the office of his supervising law partner, PAUL HUDSON, who tells Dylan that Nicole Girard has AIDS and that her parents, HENRY and NANCY GIRARD, are members of the Rev. Fletcher's original congregation. The Rev. Fletcher has asked the firm to get the Girards appointed legal guardians of their daughter so she can be committed to the hospital's psychiatric ward.

After meeting the Girards, Dylan goes to the hospital, where he discusses Nicole with Dr. Argent. Argent tells Dylan that Nicole has been HIV-positive for years and had just joined a clinical trial of a new anti-AIDS drug. Unfortunately, she developed full-blown AIDS and became deeply depressed. She suffered a severe head injury in the fall from the platform. Now conscious, she needs antipsychotic and antidepressant medication.

When he visits Nicole, however, she tells Dylan that the hospital staff has kidnapped her and that they are "sucking her blood." He thinks she's nuts, but nevertheless finds her an interesting and appealing person. As he leaves the hospital, Dylan sees KRISTIN FLETCHER, twenty-eight, daughter of the Rev. Fletcher. Kristin is an attractive redhead; he noticed her at the dedication ceremony. They chat for a while, and Dylan asks her out.

After Dylan files the guardianship petition on behalf of the Girards, he is visited by CHARLENE McCONNELL, thirty-five, Nicole's housemate and apparent lesbian lover. Charlene believes that something happened to Nicole during the clinical trial, something that made her crazy and paranoid—perhaps a side effect of the anti-AIDS drug. She asks Dylan to investigate, and when he refuses—saying he represents Nicole's parents, not Nicole—Charlene says she'll get a lawyer to represent Nicole.

That lawyer turns out to be PAMELA HOLTZ, fifty-five, a well-known feminist. Holtz tells Dylan she will be opposing the guardianship for Nicole and will be filing her own legal action to have Charlene appointed guardian.

At the same time, Dylan pursues his relationship with Kristin Fletcher. Kristin is a wild thing, not a typical minister's daughter, and is the remedy to Dylan's conservatism. He ignores warnings from his fellow lawyer and friend, BARRY SASSCER, that Kristin is too wild for him.

Dylan continues to visit Nicole in the hospital, hoping she will snap out of her paranoia—for personal reasons, he doesn't like the idea of involuntary commitment. He also has to deal with his sister, Janis, who, like her namesake, overdoses on heroin. Dylan commits her to a drug rehabilitation program.

At the court hearing on Nicole's guardianship, Pamela Holtz presents an excellent case to the female judge. Holtz has developed a unique legal theory: Charlene McConnell should have a spouse's right to be guardian because Charlene was Nicole's "domestic partner," and the state civil rights law prohibits discrimination on the basis of sexual preference. Charlene testifies movingly about her relationship with Nicole. They have been more than just lovers; they are as committed as a married couple. On cross-examination, Dylan tries to show that Charlene will profit financially from a decision in her favor, but Holtz convincingly argues her novel legal theory.

The judge, however, finally rules in Dylan's favor, appointing Henry and Nancy Girard as Nicole's guardians and empowering them to make all her medical and financial decisions.

Back in Washington, Dr. Rosati tells presidential aide Craig Olson that Nicole Girard will soon be under his care at NIH. Olson tells the president, THOMAS BANFIELD, who also seems very interested in her fate.

At his law firm, Dylan is congratulated by Paul Hudson and offered a chance to work on bigger cases. Hudson, it appears, has been using the Girard case to gain influence with Fletcher and overcome his law firm rival. Although Dylan doesn't think his victory is that impressive, he's suddenly being treated with more respect. Or is it due to his relationship with the daughter of the firm's biggest client?

Dylan celebrates by taking a ski trip with Kristin. They stay at the Rev. Fletcher's California ski condo, with the entire Fletcher extended family. Kristin introduces Dylan as her boyfriend, but this is not a popular announcement. Dylan is biracial, and Fletcher's religious sect teaches that miscegenation is sinful. Dylan encounters some marginally racist talk, but Kristin stands up for him, and so does the Rev. Fletcher—although Kristin is the family rebel, Fletcher adores and supports her.

While Dylan is in California, Mark and Linda Argent enter Nicole's hospital room. Nicole is sedated and can barely lift her head, but she watches as they stand silently by her bed. The expressions on their faces set off alarms in Nicole's brain. She tries to move, to scream, to struggle, but can't control her muscles. Linda Argent takes a previously prepared syringe out of her pocket and injects something into Nicole's IV line. Within minutes, Nicole's respirations slow to nothing.

Dylan learns from the Rev. Fletcher that Nicole Girard has died in the hospital, apparently of respiratory distress resulting from her head injuries, complicated by AIDS. This seems strange to Dylan; the last time he saw her she seemed fine, except for the heavy sedation. He certainly saw no evidence of AIDS. He is upset and decides to cut short his vacation to attend the funeral. This angers Kristin.

At Nicole's funeral, Charlene tells Dylan that he should investigate Nicole's death, and the Rev. Fletcher asks Dylan to handle Nicole's estate. Afterward, at his apartment, Dylan is assaulted by Janis's drug dealer, who believes that Janis has stolen heroin from him.

Dylan files a petition to have Henry Girard appointed as executor of Nicole's estate, expecting it will be routinely granted. He is not really surprised, however, when he is again opposed by Charlene McConnell and Pamela Holtz. McConnell also wants to be executor so that she can bring a wrongful death case against the AIDS Center and Dr. Argent. Although Dylan is now somewhat sympathetic with their goals, he must represent his client—Henry Girard—and do his best to defeat Holtz.

In support of her petition, Holtz makes the same arguments as she did during the guardianship hearing. It's an easier call for the judge this time, and she loses again. An appeal is filed immediately.

Dylan thinks it's all over, but Paul Hudson instructs him to offer McConnell $250,000 in exchange for dropping her appeal. Hudson explains that the money will be contributed by the Rev. Fletcher as a "favor" for his longtime parishioners, the Girards. The Rev. Fletcher, it seems, doesn't want to put the Girards through the "trauma" of an appeal. It doesn't make sense, but Dylan follows orders and makes the offer to Holtz, who asks him the inevitable question—why is the $250K being offered unless there is something to cover up? In any event, it doesn't take McConnell long to refuse the settlement offer. Apparently her motives are not mercenary.

In the White House, Rosati discusses Nicole's death with Olson and President Banfield, who is very distressed by the news. They encourage Rosati to find "others like her." President Banfield remembers what started it all: his brief homosexual encounter with Jason Conner, a volunteer in his last senatorial campaign. The letter Conner tried to deliver was a warning that Conner had tested positive for HIV, and feared he was a carrier when he had sex with candidate Banfield. After Conner's death, the president tested positive for HIV. It's a closely held secret known only to Rosati, Olson, and the president's wife.

Nicole Girard wakes from a drug-induced sleep in a new hospital room on the top floor of the AIDS research center. The door to the suite is solid wood—always locked—and the walls are soundproof. Two male nurses bring her food and lock her into the bedroom every night; every other day she is examined by Dr. Argent and a tube of her blood is drawn.

One day Nicole builds a pyramid of furniture to the ceiling and attempts to remove the ceiling tiles. She's almost through to the roof of the building when she feels faint, slips, and falls to the floor. When she regains consciousness, she's strapped to the bed again.

At about the same time, Pamela Holtz is brutally murdered outside a gay bar in an apparent "gay bashing" by a local motorcycle gang.

The following morning, Dylan visits Charlene McConnell, who tells him that Pamela was lured to the gay bar by someone claiming to have information about Nicole's death.

Dylan goes back to Henry Girard and convinces him that Nicole's death must be investigated. Girard signs medical authorizations allowing Dylan to obtain Nicole's medical records and autopsy report. Before Dylan can use them, however, Girard talks to the Rev. Fletcher, changes his mind, and forbids Dylan from investigating further.

Dylan feels compelled to use the medical authorizations anyway, and gets Nicole's records from the AIDS Center. There are some strange discrepancies; he consults a pathologist and learns that Nicole's autopsy report is so general it could be used in any nonviolent death.

Without telling anyone except Janis, Barry, and Kristin, Dylan travels to Washington, D.C., to the NIH. At NIH, Dylan meets Dr. Rosati and points out the discrepancies in Nicole's medical chart and autopsy. Rosati suddenly becomes very interested, and after Dylan leaves, sets up a meeting with Craig Olson. Olson is energized by this information and says he will investigate.

After the meeting with Rosati, Dylan visits the grave of his mother in a Washington suburb. She died in a particularly horrible way, while high on drugs. He is observed by a man named SKOLER and his partner.

Depressed by the visit to his mother's grave, and with some time to kill before his plane leaves for St. Louis, Dylan rents a rowing shell (he's a former varsity rower) for a workout on the

Potomac River. Skoler and his buddy follow him in a speedboat and ram his shell in an apparent murder attempt. Dylan is injured, losing the tips of several fingers.

Back home, Dylan tells Kristin everything that happened in Washington. He thinks someone—probably Argent—is trying to kill him because he is investigating Nicole's death. She thinks he's crazy. But now he's more determined than ever to find out what happened to Nicole. At the same time, Dylan becomes aware that he is being watched, or followed, or both. He buys a handgun for protection.

Dylan tells the Girards what he has learned and asks for permission to exhume Nicole's body. They agree, but then tell the Rev. Fletcher about Dylan's strange request; the Rev. Fletcher, in turn, tells Dylan's boss, Paul Hudson. Hudson hurriedly removes Dylan from Nicole's case. Now Dylan's career with the firm is in danger. At the same time, Kristin stops returning his calls.

At the same time, President Banfield's chief political rival, SENATOR OSBORNE, has independently discovered that Banfield might have AIDS. He works behind the scenes to use the information to destroy Banfield politically.

Dylan, meanwhile, is determined to get some answers. He drives to Nicole's grave site and digs up her coffin. There's a body inside—but it's not Nicole.

Returning to his apartment, Dylan is met by Craig Olson, accompanied by several government agents. Olson tells Dylan that he works for the NIH inspector general, investigating possible misuse of federal funds in clinical trials. He believes there may have been such misuse in Nicole's case. It sounds plausible, but Dylan doesn't say much, not sure he can trust Olson. Olson's visit, however, finally provides an explanation for Argent's conduct. If a lawsuit would destroy his entire program—and if he was too queasy to kill her—kidnapping made sense.

Before he can find out anything else, Dylan is kidnapped by Skoler and taken to Argent's lab. Argent shows him that Nicole is alive, and explains the reason—Nicole's body has the capacity to defeat HIV.

Her T cells are able to meet each new mutation of the virus, keeping it in check. She'll always be HIV-positive—have the antibodies—but will never develop AIDS. Argent has used Nicole's immune system to develop an AIDS drug; unfortunately, it can be produced only in small quantities. He's so close to a cure, he can practically taste the Nobel prize. It's unfortunate that Nicole must be kept prisoner, of course, but it's the only way. What if she decided to leave town? Or got hit by a truck? The freedom of one person isn't worth more than the lives of millions. In the meantime, there is enough drug to treat one or two patients: test cases.

Dylan can't understand why Argent is telling him all this, and says so. Argent points out that he will deny all of it, and Dylan has no proof. And in any event, he's sure that Dylan will never breathe a word.

Argent takes Dylan to an examination room, where a woman wearing a blond wig is receiving a blood transfusion. She looks him over, smiles, then, without a word, removes the wig. It's Kristin.

It finally hits Dylan—Kristin is one of the patients receiving the AIDS treatment made from Nicole's blood. Argent explains that Kristin has been HIV-positive for over a year. That's the reason, of course, that her father funded the AIDS Center. Dylan realizes that he has foolishly been having unprotected sex with Kristin, so he might be infected. Argent explains that as long as Dylan keeps the secret, he too will receive the medicine distilled from Nicole's blood. Otherwise—

Dylan is in shock. Why, he asks, did Argent try to have him killed in Washington? Argent denies it, clearly wondering what Dylan is talking about. In the end, Dylan agrees to keep quiet— at least until he can figure things out.

Dylan does medical research to verify Argent's story about Nicole, and finds evidence in the medical literature of patients who are immune to AIDS. He's considering his options when he notices that he is being followed—he thinks it's Olson's men. He also sees a news report that President Banfield has entered Bethesda Naval Hospital for unspecified reasons, soon after he collapsed during a White House meeting. In the background of the picture, Dylan sees—Olson! Dylan calls the White House and confirms that Olson is a presidential aide. Dylan finally figures it out: The president has AIDS, and Olson's interest in Nicole is obvious.

Dylan is tired of being reactive. He calls Olson and tells him that Nicole is still alive, being held captive by Argent, and that she is about to be moved to a new location. Then he manages to shake Olson's men, who have been following him. He goes to the hospital.

At the hospital, Dylan sneaks into the lab and frees Nicole. They have almost escaped when they are confronted by Argent and Olson. Dylan had hoped that Olson's men would keep Argent busy, but apparently they have joined forces. Dylan is about to surrender when Nicole grabs his gun and puts the barrel against her head. She threatens to kill herself unless they are allowed to leave—her life is hell, and death would be a relief. No one doubts her; and because everyone needs her, she and Dylan are released; they are immediately pursued both by the Rev. Fletcher's private police force and the Secret Service.

Eventually they take refuge with Dylan's father, HOWARD ICE, in the Ozark mountains. Howard, like his wife, has done too much LSD. Still a hippie, he lives in an abandoned mine shaft two miles from the nearest road, accompanied by a pair of vicious German shepherds.

For the next few days, Dylan and Nicole stay at the mine. Dylan realizes that he is falling in love with Nicole, and can't bring himself to tell her that he, too, is HIV-positive. At the same time, they realize they can't live in the woods forever, and that they are safer with the feds than with Argent. Dylan contacts Barry Sasscer and asks him to negotiate with the Secret Service on their behalf. Barry works out a deal: In return for allowing her blood to be used to help the president, Nicole will get $10 million and a new identity.

Before the deal can be consummated, Dylan's sister, Janis, appears at the mine. She's figured out where Dylan is hiding, and has run away from the rehab center. Unfortunately, Kristin has had Janis under surveillance and she's close behind, desperate to continue her treatments. Kristin tells Nicole that Dylan is HIV-positive, implying that Dylan has the same motives as everyone else. Dylan is furious, but before he can respond, Nicole runs out of the cabin. Kristin attempts to follow but Howard Ice blocks her way. Kristin shoots Howard, and Howard's dogs attack and kill Kristin. While this is going on, Nicole hides in the mine shaft.

Dylan and Janis are bandaging their father when the Rev. Fletcher and Argent appear. The Rev. Fletcher is brokenhearted at his daughter's death and wants immediate revenge. He orders his men to find Nicole and kill her. Argent objects, but the Rev. Fletcher tells him that he never intended to allow an AIDS cure anyway. Kristin aside, AIDS is the greatest thing that ever happened to the Rev. Fletcher—it proves his philosophy that homosexuality is ungodly. He's the one behind Pamela Holtz's death and the attacks on Dylan.

Argent, his dreams of glory shattered, attacks the Rev. Fletcher, giving Dylan and Janis the opportunity to escape. Several of the Rev. Fletcher's men chase him; Dylan hides Janis, then is himself chased by the Rev. Fletcher in his helicopter. Olson, who has been tracking the Rev. Fletcher, comes on the scene and saves Dylan's life by shooting down the Rev. Fletcher's helicopter.

Olson now is in command of the scene, but Nicole has apparently disappeared—and with her, President Banfield's last chance at a cure.

The Secret Service release Dylan, but he knows he's being watched.

Senator Osborne takes the offensive, demanding that Banfield submit to an AIDS test, and the president knows his career is finished. He commits suicide in the White House, leaving a suicide note that will destroy Osborne's career.

Dylan, fed up with law practice, takes a job as a crew coach in the Caribbean. He tests negative for AIDS, but the incubation period is such that he won't be sure he's safe for a while. Soon after, Nicole resurfaces—she has managed to make it to Switzerland, where she has claimed the $10 million put there by the president to pay for her cooperation. She visits Dylan, and tells him that half the money is his—and her blood, if necessary. In addition, she admits her love for Dylan. Whether they can have a relationship is unclear—but they will try.

Index

AAR. *See* Association of Authors'
  Representatives
Action
  describing, 179-181
  habitual, 184
Action/adventure genre, 8
Action/result writing, 144
Action mode, 142-144
  action/result writing and, 144
  chronological order and, 143
  defined, 219
Action section, 61-62
  defined, 219
  flashback as, 163
  goals of, 179
  lead's subplot in, 99, 101-103
  story line and, 92, 94
  surprise and, 106-107
  viewpoint character in, 97
  writing, 132-135
Adjectives, 180
Adverbs
  minimizing in dialogue, 152-153
  use of, 179
Age of character, 30
Agent, 2
  approaching, 201-218
  commission, 213
  compatible, 207-208
  facts about, 206
  need for, 202-203
  newcomers and, 203-204
  preparing manuscript for,
    175-176
  reading fees and, 208-209
  representation agreement, 213
  role of, 201-202
  signing with, 212-214
  targeting potential, 204-207
Andrews, V.C., 16

Appearance of character, 30-31
Aristotelian novel structure, 55-56
Association of Authors'
  Representatives (AAR), 205
Avon Books, 57
Awareness, 131-132

Background
  breaking up, 161
  on character fact list, 33
  as explanation, 159-161
  minimizing, 161
  withholding, 161
Background mode, 159-165
  defined, 219
  See also Background
Beginning
  completing, 173
  defined, 219
  plotting rest of, 103-104
  section pattern in, 108
Benchley, Peter, 16, 45
Blatty, William Peter, 16
Blythe, Hal, 35
Body language. *See* Gestures;
  Mannerisms
Bookcase, 167
Bookstore, 12-13
Bulletin board, 167

Category novel, 57
Chapters
  dividing novel into, 189-191
  length of, 190-191
Character(s)
  confidant, 44-47
  distinctive voices of, 148
  goal of, 64-65
  lead, 28-39. *See also* Lead
  limiting for story line resolution,
    117-118

main. *See* Lead
opposition, 40-43, 102
other, 40-53, 52-53, 198
romantic involvement, 48-51
section, 61-62
story line resolution and, 116
viewpoint, 94, 96, 102, 116, 120
walk-on, 181
Character fact list, 28-39
confidant, 47-48
defined, 219
lead, 30-39
opposition character, 43-44
romantic involvement, 51-52
Character type, 29
Chicago Manual of Style, The, 187
Christian genre, 8
Christie, Agatha, 16, 96
Chronological order, 143
Circumlocution, 182
Clarity, 184-185
Classic novel structure, 55-56
Cliché, 184
Clinical Trials (Steven), 223
synopsis for, 224-233
Collins, Jackie, 85
Coma (Cook), 17
Computer, 167
typing manuscript on, 187
Confidant, 44-47
character fact list, 47-48
defined, 219
in final pattern, 120-121
story line resolution for, 116
as viewpoint character, 97
Conflict, 65-67
external, 88
internal, 87-88
on section sheet, 65-67, 77-79
writing, 134-135
See also Crisis
Connector, 137-140
defined, 219
run-together, 138-139

space-break, 137-138
summary, 139-140, 145
Contemporary Authors, 206
Cook, Robin, 17
Crawford, Tad, 215
Creative flow, 174
Crisis, 15-16
brainstorming ideas for, 17-20
crisis criteria, 20-23, 219
defined, 219
intriguing, 22-23
lead's, 21-22, 64-65
story goal and, 23-26
See also Conflict

Deadlines, 174
Death Wish, 25
Description
natural, 129-130
of people, places and things,
180-181
viewpoint writing and, 181
Details, 180
Dialect, 148
Dialogue
breaking up, 151-152
distinctive voices, 148
ellipses and, 186
natural, 147-148
paragraphing, 152
punctuation, 153-154
summarizing, 154-156
tags, 148, 152
Dialogue mode, 146-157
advancing plot with, 146-147
defined, 219
See also Dialogue
*Directory of American Poets and
Fiction Writers*, 206
Draft, completing, 166-176
Du Maurier, Daphne, 16

Editing, 178-188
Editor(s)

approaching, 201-218
as businesspeople, 203
interest from, 214-215
preparing manuscript for, 175-176
submitting directly to, 214
Elements of Style, The (Strunk and White), 187
Emotion
as character's response to failure, 70
subplot creation and, 90-91
summary mode to convey, 145-146
in synopsis, 198
writing to show, 136
End, 112-126
defined, 220
no loose ends in, 118-119
Events, reporting, 145
Exorcist, The (Blatty), 16
Explanation, 159-161
External conflict, 88, 220
Eye of the Needle (Follett), 41

F-A-D (feelings/thoughts, action and dialogue), 150-151
Failure
action-section, 102
character's emotional response to, 70-71
in final pattern, 121-122
from last action section, 68, 70
on section sheet, 67, 79-81
section character's, 62
subplot creation and, 91-92
surprise as, 106-107
worsening, 109, 118
writing, 134-135
Falk, Kathryn, 57
Familiar Quotations (Bartlett's), 192
Family saga, 12
Fantasy genre, 9

Fanzines, 206
Feelings/thoughts, action and dialogue (F-A-D), 150-151
Feelings/thoughts mode, 157-159, 220
Fiction
classifications of, 8-12
subclassifications of, 8-12
See also Novel; Story
File drawers, 167
Final pattern
confidant in, 120-121
failure in, 121-122
lead and, 120
opposition character in, 121
sections of, 119-125
Final Remedy (Steven), 223
Finishing touches, 189-192
Flashback, 163-165, 220
Flowers in the Attic (Andrews), 16
Follett, Ken, 41
Foreign rights, 213

Gay/Lesbian genre, 9
Gay, Robert M., 187
Gender of character, 30
Genre
category novel, 57
Christian, 8
classifications, 8-12
crisis and, 20-21
defined, 220
family saga, 12
fantasy, 9
gay/lesbian, 9
gothic, 12
historical, 9
horror, 9
mainstream fiction, 9-10
mystery, 10
pinpointing favorite, 8
romance, 7, 10
science fiction, 11
subclassifications, 8-12

suspense, 11
western, 11
young-adult, 7, 12
your target, 13-14. *See also*
    Target genre
Gestures, 149-150
Glossary, 219-222
Goal (story)
    from last action section, 76
    new, 68, 73-75
    section, 61-62. *See also* Section
    goal
    on section sheet, 64-65
Goals (writing), 173-174
Gone With the Wind (Mitchell), 46
Gothic genre, 12
Grammar, 185-186
Guide to Literary Agents, 206

Harlequin Romance line, 30
HarperCollins Publishers, 223
Hero, 28
    See also Lead
Heroine, 28
    See also Lead
Historical fiction, 9
Historical romance
    Point of Hopelessness in, 122-123
    viewpoint characters in, 96
Hollywood Wives (Collins), 85
Hopelessness, Point of, 122-124
Hopkins, Jane Ellice, 217
Horror genre
    subclassifications of, 9
    as target genre, 13
How to Write Mysteries (OCork),
    57
*How to Write a Romance and Get
    It Published* (Falk), 57

Idea. *See* Story idea
Internal conflict, 87-88, 220
*International Authors and
    Writers Who's Who*, 206

Interweaving story lines, 83-104

James, P.D., 17
Jaws (Benchley), 16, 45

Kenyon, Sherrilyn, 35

Lead
    age of, 17
    character's connection to, 29
    creating, 28-39
    crisis and, 21-22
    defined, 220
    defining, 16-17, 28-39
    in final pattern, 120
    goal of, 23-26, 64-65
    main story line resolution, 116
    number of sections for, 102
    opposition character and, 42-43,
        118
    romantic involvement of, 48-51
    section failure, 62
    subplot of, 101-103, 220
    subplot creation for, 86-92
    subplot resolution, 116
    in synopsis, 196-198
Length
    of chapters, 190-191
    ideal novel, 56-58
    word, 222
Letter, query. *See* Query letter
Library, 12-13
Line, 220
Literary agent, 2
    See also Agent
Literary Market Place (*LMP*), 206
LMP. See Literary Market Place
Locus, 206
Lutz, John, 84
Lyons, Tony, 215

Main story line, 220
    See also Story line
Mainstream fiction, 9-10

Mannerisms, 32
Manuscript
  cover letter with, 212
  finishing touches on, 189-192
  length of, 56-57
  polishing, 177-192
  preparing professional, 175-176
  revising and editing, 178-179
  self-editing, 179-186
  translating into synopsis,
    196-200
  unsolicited, 209
Market, adapting, 12-13
Marketing, 193-233
  agent and, 201
*Merriam-Webster's Collegiate
  Dictionary*, 187
Metaphor, 180
Middle
  completing, 173
  crafting, 107
  defined, 220
  first sections in, 109
Misplaced modifiers, 185
Mitchell, Margaret, 46
Mode
  action, 142-144
  awareness of, 165
  background, 159-165
  dialogue, 146-157
  feelings/thoughts, 157-159
  summary, 144-146
Motivation
  lead's, 24
  in synopsis, 198
Murder on the Orient Express
  (Christie), 16
Murder of Roger Ackroyd, The
  (Christie), 96
My Cousin Rachel (Du Maurier),
  16
Mystery genre, 10
Mystery Scene, 206
Mystery Writer's Sourcebook, 206

Naming character, 33-34
Negotiation, with editor, 214-215
New Testament, 192
Novel
  beginning, 103-104, 108, 173, 219
  classic structure of, 55-56
  ending, 112-126, 220
  finding perfect, 6-14
  ideal length of, 56-58
  marketing your, 193-233
  middle, 107, 109, 173, 220
  See also Fiction; Story
NovelMaster, 59

OCork, Shannon, 57
Old Testament, 192
Opposition, 40-43
  action-section failure and, 102
  defined, 220
  in final pattern, 121
  limiting lead's options, 118
  story line resolution for, 116
  as viewpoint character, 96-97

Page(s)
  numbering, 175
  title, 192
Paragraphs
  avoiding long, 186
  dialogue and, 152
Pattern
  failure in, 121
  final, 119-125
  section, 108, 114-115
  of story lines, 101
Perceptions, viewpoint and, 132
Personality, 32-33
Planning for success, 5-53
Plotting
  advancing with dialogue mode,
    146-147
  classic structure, 55-56
  complete guide to, 54-126
  ideal novel length, 56-58

rest of beginning, 103-104
    tools for, 58-61
Poetics (Aristotle), 55
Point of Hopelessness, 122-124,
    220
Polishing your manuscript, 177-192
Possession
    as crisis goal, 24
    lead's subplot and, 88-90
Possessives, 181
Precision, 184-185
Presumed Innocent (Turow), 17
Price, Nancy, 41
Prime of Miss Jean Brodie, The
    (Spark), 42
Printer, 167
Professional manuscript, 175-176
Pronouns, 186
Proposal, producing knockout,
    194-200
Publishers
    agents and, 202-203
    guidelines, 30
    See also specific publishers
Publishers Weekly, 206
Punctuation
    dialogue, 153-154
    ellipses, 186
    exclamation points, 186
    in manuscript, 175-176

Qualifiers, 182
Query letter, 209-212
    sample, 211
Quotas, writing, 173-174

Rational phase, 63, 71-73
Reaction section, 63
    defined, 220
    logical, 179
    new goal or, 68
    Point of Hopelessness as,
        122-124
    time in, 136-137

    writing, 135-137
Reader
    surprising, 105-111
    updating, 133-134
    writer as, 7-8
Reading fees, 208-209
Redundancy, 181, 183
Rejection, 215-216
Relief, 24
Representation agreement, 213
Revising, 178-179
Romance genre
    insincere effort at, 7
    length of books in, 56-57
    subclassifications of, 10
    tip sheet for, 30
    See also Historical romance
Romantic involvement, 48-51
    character fact list, 50-52
    defined, 221
    final section patterns and,
        114-115
    lead's subplot and, 86-90
    story line resolution for, 116
    as viewpoint character, 96
    wrap-up for, 124-125
Romantic Times, 206
Run-together connector, 138-139,
    221

Saving Act, 124, 221
Schedule, writing, 170-172
Science fiction, 11
*Science Fiction and Fantasy
    Writer's Sourcebook*, 206
Section(s)
    action, 61-62
    connecting in summary mode,
        145
    defined, 58, 221
    distribution in NovelMaster, 59
    of final pattern, 119-125
    reaction, 63, 122-124
    writing, 172-173

Section character, 221
Section goal
    defined, 221
    new, 73-75
Section pattern
    in beginning of novel, 108
    final, 114-115. *See also* Final
        pattern
Section sheet(s), 58-61
    blank, 60
    defined, 221
    four samples, 64-82
    using, 64
    writing with, 172
Self-editing, 179-186
Senses, 181
Sentence overload, 186
Shakespeare, 192
Silhouette Romances, 30, 56-57
Simile, 180
Simplicity, 181-184
Skillin, Marjorie E., 187
Slugline, 175
Something About the Author, 206
Space-break connector, 137-138,
    221
Spark, Muriel, 42
Speech pattern, 32
    See also Dialect; Dialogue
Sleeping With the Enemy (Price),
    41
Spelling checker, 187
Steven, Daniel, 223
Story
    beginning, 103-104, 108, 173, 219
    end, 112-126
    middle, 107, 109-110
    See also Fiction; Novel
Story goal, 23-26
    on character fact list, 29
    defined, 221
Story goal criteria, 221
Story idea, 26-27
    defined, 221

shaping your, 15-27
Story line(s)
    defined, 221
    guidelines for juggling, 101-103
    interweaving, 83-104
    involving other characters, 84-85
    lead's main, 120
    pattern of, 101
    resolution of, 116
    returning to main, 92, 94
    rotating, 102
Strunk, William, Jr., 187
Style, 185-186
Subplot(s)
    advantages of, 83-86
    defined, 221
    lead's, 86-92, 101-103, 116, 120
    other characters', 94, 96-97
    resolution of, 116
    romantic, 86-87
Success, planning for, 5-53
Summary
    action mode and, 144
    for dialogue, 154-156
Summary connector, 139-140, 221
Summary mode, 144-146, 222
Supplies, 168-169
Supposes
    defined, 222
    where to find, 17-20
    See also Crisis
Surprise, 105-111
    defined, 222
    as failure, 106
    first, 106-110
    second, 110
    third, 110-111
Suspense genre, 11
Sweet, Charlie, 35
SWF Seeks Same (Lutz), 84
Synopsis
    basics of writing, 195-196
    defined, 222
    mechanics of, 194-195

polishing, 200
with query letter, 210
sample, 223-233
translating manuscript into,
    196-200

Tags
    dialogue, 148, 152
    feelings/thoughts and, 157-158
Tangents, 109-110
Target genre, 13-14
    crisis appropriate for, 20-21
    gender requirement in, 16
    title and, 191-192
Thriller, 123-124
Time
    extended period of, 145
    in reaction section, 136-137
    tracking, 179
Tip sheet, 30, 222
Title, 191-192
Title page, 192
Turow, Scott, 17
Twain, Mark, 180

Unsolicited submission, 209
Updating, 133-134
Usage (word), 185-186

Viewpoint
    awareness and, 131-132
    as filter, 130-131
    perceptions in, 132
Viewpoint character(s), 94, 96
    action-section failure and, 102

defined, 222
in final pattern, 120
story line resolution for, 116
Viewpoint writing, 128-132
    defined, 222
    descriptions and, 181
    viewpoint as filter, 130-131
    See also Viewpoint
Voltaire, 180

Weather, 180
Western genre, 11
White, E.B., 187
*Who's Who in Writers, Editors,
    and Poets*, 206
Word length, 222
Word processor, 167
    typing manuscript on, 187
Words Into Type (Skillin and Gay),
    187
Work space, 166-170
Worst Failure, defined, 222
Wrap-up, 124-125, 222
Writer's Digest Books, 206, 215
*Writer's Digest Character
    Naming Sourcebook*
    (Kenyon), 35
Writers Directory, 206
Writer's Legal Guide, The
    (Crawford and Lyons), 215
Writing
    as journey, 217
    schedule, 170-172
    work space for, 166-170

Young adult genre, 7, 12

For Further Information

If you would like information on either The Evan Marshall Agency or The Marshall Plan Novel-Writing Workshops, please contact

The Evan Marshall Agency/
The Marshall Plan Novel-Writing Workshops
Six Tristam Place
Pine Brook, New Jersey 07058-9445
Telephone: (973) 882-1122
Fax: (973) 882-3099
E-mail: evanmarshall@thenovelist.com
Web: www.thenovelist.com

Please send us any publishing success stories, inspirational stories or successful writing strategies you have derived from using *The Marshall Plan* so we can share them with others in future books and workshops.